D0793167

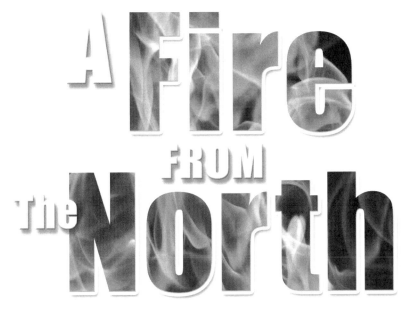

A Fire from the North

A Vision of Revival for America

All correspondence to the author should be sent to:

Juan Francisco
247 Valley St.
Providence, RI 02909

(401) 421-7600
Pastorfrco@cox.net

ISBN: 978-0-942507-26-3
E-book ISBN: 978-0-942507-27-0

A Fire from the North: A Vision of Revival for America

Printed in the United States of America
Published by **Deeper Revelation Books**
Revealing "the deep things of God" (1 Cor. 2:10)
P.O. Box 4260 ● Cleveland, TN 37320-4260
Phone: 423-478-2843 ● Fax: 423-479-2980
Website: www.deeperrevelationbooks.org

Wholesalers and bookstores should direct their orders to Deeper Revelation Books. Refer to the website for an online catalog of all books published by Deeper Revelation Books, as well as distribution information.

Deeper Revelation Books assists Christian authors in publishing and distributing their books. Final responsibility for design, content, permissions, editorial accuracy, and doctrinal views, either expressed or implied, belongs to the author.

A Fire
FROM
The North

A Vision of Revival for America

Juan Francisco

Dedications

I dedicate this book first to the One who gave His life for me on a cross, my LORD and Savior Jesus Christ. Next, I want to acknowledge all the wonderful people of Minnesota and North and South Dakota. Also, I want to honor and recognize my loving parents, my faithful and loving wife, Debbie, and the congregation of the Door of Refuge Assemblies of God Church, which I am privileged to pastor. Finally, this book is also dedicated to my children, Alexandra, Pearla, and Amaris, and my grandchildren, David, Leilani, and Christian.

Table of Contents

Introduction

All indications point to a strong spiritual revival that is about to overtake the entire land of the United States of America. For many of us who have been witnesses to the most recent catastrophic events in American History, such a revelation fills us with hope and positive expectations. We are assured by God that even though we might have been going through some tough times as a nation, help is on the way.

As negative as the recent events in our nation have been, one cannot help but remember God's unfailing promises. He reminds us through the words of the Apostle Paul, *In all things God works for the good of those who love Him, who have been called according to His purpose.* (Rom. 8:28)

It is my belief that America has gradually and persistently deviated from the godly principles that helped make this a strong and righteous nation. That has set in motion a chain of events which has forced our society as a whole to re-examine itself in terms of its values and domestic and foreign policy. God has permitted it to spiral downward from one crisis to another.

In a society where over 80% of its population professes to be Christian, it's no wonder that at the very first sign of serious national danger, pollsters found a dramatic increase of people seeking answers and a sense of security by reaching back to their spiritual heritage. Such was the case immediately after the September 11 attack on America in 2001. Surveys immediately after that traumatic event found a dramatic increase in church attendance. A few weeks later, things seemed to go back to normal. Such is the fickle nature of spiritual commitment in America today.

During the Second World War, the world witnessed a sleeping giant rise on the world scene at a critical time, with power and resolve. Out of that experience, the United States received the recognition of a super power. Where did that power come from? I believe that power came from God.

The United States was called by God to fulfill a destiny that was meant to go far and beyond the historical interpretation of the concept of Manifest Destiny. As long as this nation saw itself fulfilling God's call to serve as a beacon of God's light to the world, God's blessing accompanied its admirable growth and development as a nation. However, when such success began to awaken feelings of self-reliance and pride, a distancing from God became the expected result.

If there is one thing the average Christian in America can agree upon, it is this—the church in America, and the American people as a whole, have experienced a remarkable decline in terms of their spiritual zeal. The streams of believers crying out for revival have become a tremendous force which is slowly turning into a mighty river of repentance and renewal throughout the land.

The oppression of the forces of darkness that have been felt in this nation can only be attributed to the gradual absence of light. With good reason Jesus reminds us:

"You are the salt of the earth. But if the salt loses its saltiness, how can it be made salty again? It is no longer good for anything, except to be thrown out and trampled by men. You are the light of the world. A city on a hill cannot be hidden. Neither do people light a lamp and put it under a bowl. Instead they put it on its stand, and it gives light to everyone in the house. In the same way, let your light shine before men, that they may see your good deeds and praise your Father in heaven." (Mt. 5:13-16)

One of the most important properties and utilities of salt is its ability to inhibit flesh from corruption. There is something very special about this declaration. As long as the church remains engaged in her responsibility in obedience to Jesus' Great Commission mandate, this world cannot deteriorate into complete chaos and darkness.

Thankfully, God is not going to leave us without direction and hope. Through many different yielded vessels, the LORD has been speaking to anyone who wants to hear. The welcome increases in the prophetic and other important gifts of the Spirit, together with the eternal, written Word of God, are real tangible evidences that we have not been left to fend for ourselves.

This book is meant to be one of those prophetic voices in this great time of need that cry out in the dessert of complacency and unbelief of our modern times. This book is a revelation of a powerful revival that is about to sweep the United States of America. It was given to the writer in a vision in June of 1998.

It is my prayer that as you read this book, you can receive this vision and believe that God is in the process of doing a mighty big thing in this country. This book is written at a time when many men and women of God with powerful anointed ministries have been used by God to confirm the vision you are about to receive. Can you believe?

CHAPTER 1

A Brief Historical Background

AN ISLAND IN CRISIS

Before proceeding any further, I would like to provide the reader with some historical background about myself that will help give you perspective on this journey into the supernatural. The brief reference to the historical background that led to our departure from the Dominican Republic is only a bird's-eye view of a much larger historical picture.

The year 1965 was a turning point for me and my family as well as the people of the Dominican Republic, my native land. It was during that year that a fierce, popular uprising overtook the peace of the Dominican people. The revolt of the people became better known as the Revolution of 1965. The Dominican Republic shares the island of Hispaniola together with Haiti in the Caribbean. Its political history is filled with instability and foreign domination. During the 1920's, under the leadership of a U.S. trained "Dominican National Guard" officer named Rafael Trujillo Molina, a dictatorship was established which lasted for 30 years. It ended with the assassination of the dictator on May 30, 1961. (amteword press, 2009)[1]

---

[1] "Let Me Explain, The 1965 Revolution in the Dominican Republic," amtewordpress, July 30, 2009, http://amte.wordpress.com/2009/07/30/the-1965-revolution-in-the-dominican-republic/

A period of great expectation and promise began with that event for the Dominican people. However, absent the experience in governing a nation with tender aspirations towards democracy, and the pressure that was placed on the Island by the United States' determination to protect its national interest, it became clear that the developing young nation had only entered a new phase of instability. Its struggle for normalcy was marred by numerous military takeovers which took the country from one crisis to another.

Awakened with a new sense of nationalism and aspirations of independence, and fueled by U.S. imperialism, and coupled with the successful uprising in Cuba in the mid 1900's, the Dominican people elected Dr. Juan Bosch as the first democratically elected president in Dominican history in 1962. From the outset, the election of President Bosch was marred with allegations of communist infiltration and manipulations of Dominican politics. Unfortunately, Dr. Bosch's rhetoric during the campaign process, and the policies of his newly elected government did nothing to quell suspicion from critics both internally and abroad, mainly within the United States government.

THE BOILING POINT

Allegations of communist influence in Dominican politics, and the unwillingness of Dr. Bosch to conform to certain policies of the U.S. Government, reached its boiling point in September of 1963. The new government policy for agrarian reform and the exercise of its new foreign policy had convinced certain influential sectors of the Dominican population, including certain sectors of the armed forces, that the country was in eminent danger of a communist takeover. Certainly the intelligence provided by the United States played a major role in the arrival at such conclusions. Suddenly and unexpectedly, the first democratically elected Government was over. President Bosch was quietly flown to the neighboring island of Puerto Rico, where he maintained his claim to the presidency as dictated by the Dominican people in a fairly free election.

TROUBLE IN PARADISE

After the ouster of Dr. Bosch, the U.S. helped establish a governing body that became better known as "the Triumvirate", under the leadership of a general by the name of Elias Wessin of the Armed Forces Training Center or "CEFA". The clear evidence that the armed forces perceived themselves as fighting a communist insurrection is found in the fact that one of the very first actions taken by the Triumvirate was to outlaw the Marxist doctrine of communism. These communist groups, they felt, were attempting to take over the country. However, it did not take long before everyone began to realize that this was an insurrection of the people which had been galvanized by the ouster of their first popularly elected president. What the people were most upset about was the apparent disregard with which the U.S. Government was treating their very strong sentiments for democracy. (Sanchez, 2010)[2]

Some in the armed forces refused to obey orders to fight against the people. Such was the case with General Renato Malagón Montesano, my uncle, who was one of the generals in charge at the San Isidro Air Force Base at the time. People, nonetheless, were fighting and dying by the thousands. As the civil war progressed, it appeared that the populace was gaining much ground.

The state of affairs in neighborhoods was horrendous. Just about every day we heard news of a neighbor who had been killed. The crying of women left as widows and their children and friends, could be heard from neighborhood to neighborhood. Such sounds of sorrow and pain, as well as the smell of death, imprinted in my psyche a memory strong enough to last a life time.

What bullets could not accomplish, hunger threatened to finish. My older brother, Samuel, was forced to join the groups of young men who would venture into the city in search for food. Unfortunately, the only way to find some food or water

---

[2] Filiberto Cruz Sánchez, <u>Historia de la República Dominicana</u> (Editorial El Nuevo Diario, S.A., 2010) 335-343

was to risk ones' life as the hungry mobs stormed into food stores and supermarkets. Many of them were shot on the spot. We were always so worried that one day my brother would not return home, but would become another casualty of the war. Miraculously, he always returned safe and sound, and was able to find food for the family. (Read Psalm 91)

THE SOUND OF THUNDER

It became evident to our more well-to-do part of the family that we would not be able to survive for long where we lived. This was assumed for two primary reasons. First, we did not have a regular source of food. Second, if anyone fighting the military realized that we were directly related to high ranking officials of the armed forces, we would have been in grave danger.

Our situation got more desperate as water, which was scarce on a regular basis in our neighborhood, stopped flowing altogether. Samuel and I risked our lives and went to get water from a spring near the Ozama River. My brother could not believe that we'd find drinkable water at the edge of the river that was almost as salty as the ocean itself, because the Ozama River begins its final descent into the Caribbean Sea not too far from there. I had discovered the ground spring some years earlier as I ventured in that area with my childhood friends enjoying the wonderful sights, sounds, and smells of the tropical wild country. Those were very wonderful years.

In any event, as my brother and I reached the site in question, we were thrilled to see that wonderful burst of water spring from the ground. After a test drink, we proceeded quickly to fill our cans with water. As we were doing so, two men came out of the bushes with weapons in hand. They wore security guard uniforms which were torn and dirty. As they approached frantically from the bushes, they cried out to us to leave the area immediately since they were being pursued by a mob that had already killed two or three other security guards. The farm that they were guarding had been overrun by the mob.

Of course, we got very nervous and scared. At first we thought we were going to get killed by those men. As we ran for our lives along a crooked and narrow path between a river and the foot of a mountain, we didn't know what to do. Do we get rid of the water and run? But we had walked so far to get the water that it didn't seem fair to let it go, even if it saved our lives. There was no water anywhere to be found in our neighborhood. Samuel was running in front of me. It was difficult to run carrying the pales of water on our shoulders. Samuel cried out to me, "Do I get rid of the water?" I answered, "Go ahead"! Samuel was so nervous that he threw his pale of water in front of me, forgetting that I was running right behind him. It was impossible for me to avoid the can in front of me, so I tripped and fell to the ground face down. As I was falling, I fought to save the only water left which I was carrying and in so doing dislocated my left index finger. To this day it exhibits a curvature when extended, which I humorously refer to as my "scar of war."

Approaching our home, we stood in horror and silence on the side of the street as we saw a car at high speed come to an abrupt halt right in front of our house. Three heavily armed men jumped out of the car. One of them ran into our house. My brother and I looked at each other wondering what to do. We were quick to agree; if those men had been sent to kill our family, they would have to kill us as well.

We walked rapidly toward the house. It was a very dangerous situation. As we got closer, we were able to see that the car was a military vehicle. In fact, it looked like the car that my uncle, the general, used for official duties. Nonetheless, we weren't sure. We expected to be shot at any moment. As we approached the house, the soldiers fixed their sights straight toward us. They intercepted us with weapons drawn, stopped us, and asked us to identify ourselves, which we promptly did. It was not until that point that they identified themselves as my uncle's body guards who had been sent to rescue us from the eminent danger our extended family thought we were in.

I was ready to go with them. The plan was to take us to the nearest air force base where my uncle's headquarters were located. My mother, however, was very upset about the whole incident and told the guards that she felt more concerned about what could happen to us now that neighbors knew with certainty that we were related to the military. She refused to go. The uniformed soldiers, like a scene from Mission Impossible, ran fast to their vehicle and disappeared at a very high speed. I think that our hearts were beating as fast as that car was driving away.

In retrospect, my mother's refusal to go at first was more than justified. As it turned out, the rebel forces had targeted the military air base site in question and had come very close to overtaking it by force. If that would have happened, it was very likely that most of the military personnel at the air force site would have been killed.

No more than three days had gone by when the incident repeated itself. Except, this time, the soldiers had been given instructions from my uncle not to accept any arguments or refusal. The decision had been made. We were going to the base, whether we liked it or not. And so we did.

We were to stay in my uncle's house until the public turmoil subsided. However, we were also under the distinct impression that the military families at the base were as scared as the people we had left behind in our neighborhood. Conversations among family members revealed great concern that the "rebels" were planning to overrun the base. The military personnel available were facing a very difficult challenge. Reports from credible sources placed the mobs in close proximity to the military base where we were staying.

What we didn't know was there was a plan that had been set in motion by the military leadership in the country to involve American forces in the conflict. That plan became evident only a few days into our stay at the base. Early one morning in 1965, residents at the base were rudely awakened by the thundering sounds of military aircraft. We overheard the roars of helicopters, airplanes, and other military equipment and personnel. We were told by our aunt that there was no need for concern, because the noise we were hearing was the arrival of the United States Marines. They came at the request of the arm forces of the Dominican Republic to help put an end to the insurrection, which by then had gotten quite out of hand from the military assessments.

BACK TO THE HOOD

The U.S. Marines did help quench the rebellion, but not without considerable casualties to all sides involved. The time came when it was safe for us to return to our neighborhood. It took some time for things to return to "normal." We were able to bring with us from the base a reasonable supply of military food rations which helped us survive for a few weeks.

The aftermath of the revolution was plagued with higher unemployment and other hardships. In addition, many felt insecure due to the possibility of retaliation. Our situation was not as desperate as many other families because my father had already been in the United States two years before the revolution broke out. Every now and then, he was able to send us some money to take care of our needs. We followed suit in the winter of 1968, and travelled via Puerto Rico to the United States.

CHAPTER 2

Living in the USA

A TURBULENT FLIGHT

D uring the winter of 1968, my mother, four boys and one girl, boarded a plane scheduled to land at the John F. Kennedy Airport in New York. However, the chilly welcoming effect of a powerful blizzard forced us to land in Washington, D. C. The turbulent flight made some people on the plane sick. My mother was praying and singing Christian songs. All this was a surreal experience for me since we had something similar happen on our flight from the Dominican Republic to Puerto Rico. The latter was even scarier, given that our two engine plane almost went down into the turbulent waters of the Caribbean Sea.

As we were approaching the airport in Washington, D. C., a newspaper reporter who was seated next to me asked me if I planned to leave the plane with the clothing I had on. According to my calculation, I thought I was overdressed, wearing a sweater I had been given by a family member in Puerto Rico. I responded that I thought I would be fine. He pulled out his coat and showed it to me and told me that it was so cold outside of the plane that I needed to have one of those on. Believe it or not, I was still in disbelief. Apparently, I was so accustomed to the tropical lifestyle that I could not conceive that people could actually survive under such conditions that required the heavy winter clothing the concerned reporter was trying to introduce me to.

When the plane landed, I noticed the ground personnel were wearing ski masks over their faces. I also noticed that there was smoke coming out of their mouths and nostrils. I tried to figure out where they were holding their cigarettes. Much to my dismay and confusion, I could not tell that they were smoking at all. Then it began to dawn on me that I was in serious trouble.

As we exited the plane into a bus which transported us to the terminal, I felt for the first time the merciless impact of the freezing air. I panicked for a moment and almost tried to go back into the airplane, but the line of people exiting didn't permit such an ill-conceived strategy. I seriously thought I wouldn't survive even the transfer from the plane to the bus. Being the polite young man that my parents raised me up to be, I wouldn't normally dare to cut in line, but it surely crossed my mind at that moment.

As the bus journey from Washington to New York City got underway, the most curious scenery began to catch my attention. I noticed that there was not one single tree, except for pine trees, that displayed any green leaves. All the trees looked dried and dead. It was, to me, a most depressing scene. Something wasn't right and needed an explanation. How could it be that all the trees would be dead? What kind of country was the United States of America? Somehow in conversations I became aware that in the cold climates the trees lost their leaves in the winter. My, what a relief!

Life in the Ghetto

We were processed again through customs at the J. F. Kennedy Airport. When we came out, an uncle of mine and his family was waiting for us. Fortunately, they had coats for us. They were not necessarily our size, but we were grateful that we didn't have to go on the streets of New York City without proper clothing.

The amount of snow in the streets of New York was mind boggling. After the snow trucks cleared the streets, there were lines of parked cars that appeared to have been buried. It was a very intimidating scene for a young man from a tropical island. At the same time, a feeling of adventure and intrigue took over my senses. I tried to convince myself that, just as I was able to survive through a revolution, I should be able to survive the mean streets of New York. Little did I know things were about to get worse.

When we arrived at our destination, I began to worry. We first lived in the Western part of the Bronx with my uncle for a short period of time. We soon moved to the East side of the Bronx—Talk about culture shock! The streets of the Bronx were cold, indifferent, and outright dangerous. I really began to wonder if we could survive there. My father owned a barbershop at the front of a five-story edifice ("buildings" as they were called there) and we lived on the third floor.

We began to attend a Pentecostal church in the neighborhood which was conveniently located nearby. I only attended that church because I felt closed in at home and afraid to venture too far away from home, especially since I didn't know my way around very well. Besides, I liked the pastors so I gradually began attending the church more frequently. That church experience came to an abrupt halt that same winter of 1968. That great church building caught on fire and burned down. We rushed to the church site and found only the ruins of what once was a beautiful church.

I was very disappointed and withdrew quickly from church life. The pastors were relocated and the church was never rebuilt at that location. But God was dealing with me. I was invited once to a church youth rally in another section of the Bronx. I remember that I sat on the last pew. A man was preaching. The message was strong and powerful. Under conviction, I began to cry. When the altar call was given, I didn't need assistance to come forward because I realized how much I needed forgiveness and how much I needed God in my life.

CHAPTER 3

The Beginning of a Calling

A New Life Begins

That day, in the last part of the winter of 1968, I was born again. I was sixteen years old. The joy of my new-found life in Christ was soon to be tested. I began to witness about Christ to whoever was willing to listen. That love for the lost soon got me into trouble.

Right next door to our apartment lived two young ladies to whom we witnessed about the need for salvation. They became very interested in our message. However, one of the girls' boyfriend, unbeknown to us, was a powerful gang leader who was feared in the neighborhood for his violent history. He found out about me and became very jealous thinking that I was romantically interested in that young lady.

He and his friends started showing up at the apartment complex and waiting at the door. When I came down to go to church, or for any other reason, he and his friends would challenge me to fight. When I ignored them, they'd spit at my feet and insult me with foul language. But I had the love of God in my heart. I knew it because if they would have challenged me before my conversion, I would have preferred to fight to the death. Such was my pride that I brought with me from my homeland where I was well known as a quiet but tough guy.

DEMONS NEXT DOOR

There is no question that we were very intimidated by those guys. It was enough to keep us from even talking to those girls about the Gospel. We just kept to ourselves in the apartment building. However, even that relative peace would be challenged before long.

One late afternoon, after I settled in the house fresh from school, my brother, Samuel, and I heard a loud and persistent knock on our door. In our building, the front door was strong enough to protect a fortress. There was a metal pole which rested in a hole on the floor that was finished inside with metal. The top of the security pole then was placed on a metal plate at the center of the door. It was called a "poly lock." The door itself was finished with metal. In addition to that, there were at least two heavy duty dead bolts and a peep site. That pretty much tells you the kind of neighborhood we were living in.

We ignored the persistent knock on the door for a bit. The urgency of the knock made our hearts beat fast because we knew there was something wrong. Our instincts told us that it would not be a good idea to open that door no matter what. However, we heard a female voice coming from the other side. I recognized the voice as one of the two sisters next door. I suggested to my brother that we should at least see what she wanted. My brother was emphatic not to even approach that door. I'm sure that there have been cases of people being shot in situations such as that while approaching a door in that neighborhood.

Strangely, I felt a certain impulse to get closer and listen to her cry. As I approached the door, my heart pounded in my chest. I peeked through the peep site and confirmed that it was one of the two sisters. Without opening the door, I coached her to calm down and to speak slower so that I could understand what she was trying to say.

I understood her to say that her sister was in her apartment and needed help. She told me that her sister was possessed by a devil. She urged me to come and help her sister because she was afraid of what might happen. I went back to the living room and told my brother that we should go and help her. My brother declined. You see, my brother had not yet reconciled his life with Jesus, so I think he did not feel ready for such a spiritual confrontation.

I, on the other hand, felt a certain excitement to go. I felt a power with me that was superior to any other. I felt the presence of the Holy Spirit and I also felt that I heard His voice assuring me of a victory over the forces of darkness. To me, all this was new and exhilarating. I'd never before had an encounter with a demonic manifestation. So I grabbed my Bible and told my brother, "I will go."

I opened the door with caution. The thought crossed my mind that we could have been set up for an ambush by the gang leader. I knew too well what could happen if the boyfriend found me in that apartment alone with those two young ladies. Nonetheless, I had a certain feeling of invincibility that was very real and comforting. The young lady led me to the apartment. She seemed very agitated but she was no longer screaming.

As I entered the apartment, I came face to face with a very intimidating and surreal scene. Inside, there was a bedroom that was painted black on one side with a satanic altar. There was a table at the altar with lit candles and other objects of satanic worship. There was also a picture, upside down of the Archangel Michael subduing Satan, who was depicted with horns and oversized, bat-like wings. His arms were in a defensive posture covering his face as he prepared to receive a mortal blow from Saint Michael's sword. The room was dark and eerie. There was a smell of incense coming from the room.

To be honest, after I had entered that apartment, I wasn't sure if I had done the right thing. I was a mere youth, 16 years old, and recently reconciled into the church! Wasn't this the kind of stuff that should be done by spiritual grown-ups? As I turned towards the possessed girl who was lying on a couch, things got even more intimidating.

The girl looked pale white, as if she was dead. There was no movement from her at all. Her eyes were rolled over showing only white. Her head was leaned backwards, and her body was as tense as a corpse. Her scared sister was in the room watching my movements attentively. I think she noticed that I was beginning to show that I was a bit shaken myself. As I approached the couch I said to myself, "OK, now what do I do?" After many years of ministry, as I look back on that moment, I can't help but marvel at God's grace and faithfulness as He used me on that day. Remember, I was only 16 years old at the time.

In any event, I stood in front of the possessed girl, Bible in hand, and made a silent prayer for Holy Spirit's direction. I felt the proper thing to do at that point was to simply open up the Bible to the New Testament. I knew that I would be greatly relieved if I could find a specific scripture that dealt with demon possession but the scripture was not clear in my mind. So I opened the Bible in the Book of Mark and, on the very first try, I was able to locate the narration of the possessed man of Gadara (Mark 5:1-19).

As I began to read the scripture aloud, the young lady on the couch began to show signs of life, but her eyes were still white and her body was extremely tense. I was almost finished reading the scripture when I heard a moaning sound coming from her. It was a man's deep voice, not the voice I knew was hers. It was a sound straight from hell. The deep male voice began to say a name. At first, I couldn't quite understand it. But then I was able to make it out. It sounded as if the spirit was repeating the name "Sammy". "Who is Sammy?" I asked. The reason I asked the question was my brother's name is also Sammy, and I was taking what I thought was a demonic threat to my brother a bit personal. Before I could ask again, the other sister interrupted me and explained that Sammy was their mother's boyfriend. What a relief I felt! Meanwhile, the demon continued to repeat the name.

I ignored its uttering and proceeded with the deliverance. As I continued to read the scripture, the girl began to twist and turn while the demon continued to voice unintelligible utterances. At times, I felt like stopping and running for my life. But I stood my ground and did not allow fear get the best of me.

When I finished reading the scripture, I felt emboldened. Holding my Bible in my left hand and looking straight into the girls' face, I commanded the demon to come out of her immediately in the name of Jesus, never to return to that body again! I said it with authority and without fear. At that point, the girl's body bent upward, only her shoulders and ankles making contact with the sofa. Her eyes began to bulge and appeared almost ready to come out of their sockets. Her body remained bent and her eyes rolled over, not blinking at all. I repeated the command. The demon seemed to want to break that poor girl's body in half. She began to foam from her mouth. The demon was doing everything in its power to resist, but the liberating power of the risen Christ was too strong! Just when it looked as if the demon would have its way by killing that girl, the spirit loosened its grip over her. Her body suddenly straightened out on the couch. There was a moment of silence. I continued to pray. But I sensed in my spirit that the liberation had occurred! Praise God!

The girl regained consciousness immediately and began to ask what had happened. I took the opportunity to lead her to Christ as I explained to her how the power of Jesus freed her from demonic bondage.

In this very dramatic way, my initiation into the deliverance ministry began. That was on-the-job training of the scariest type. I learned many important lessons that later would become useful to me in the ministry of liberation. One of the most important was to trust the Holy Spirit even in the most challenging moments. God was gracious to a young man who was full of faith and that would not back down from demonic forces. Later in ministry those lessons would prove extremely helpful.

The hatred from that gang against us did not relent. If anything, it intensified. One night as my brother and I were at my father's barbershop, the gang leader showed up with ten other members. Without any provocation, they came swinging at us. We did the best we could to protect and defend ourselves, but it was two against ten, and we were no match for these tough guys full of hate. We were very skilled at fighting, especially my brother Samuel who won most of his fist fights back at home, even when facing stronger adversaries. He was highly respected for his boxing skills. But to be frank with you, I was praying to God for help because we knew we were grossly outnumbered.

Just when the gang members had gotten a hold of us, the help came. A Puerto Rican businessman, who owned a small restaurant next to my father's barbershop, came out brandishing a nickel plated, .38 revolver. He screamed from the top of his lungs and said: "If you don't let them go, someone is going to die here tonight!" The gang knew he was serious and they immediately let us go with threats of further violence against us.

We went back to our apartment but were very concerned about my father's business and his safety. The next day the problem continued. Members of the gang, including the leader, returned and this time they claimed that nothing would stop them. They came in front of our apartment and began to bang on the door. They were calling us cowards and enticing us to come out. They threatened to set the apartment on fire and indicated that they had weapons with them. We didn't have a telephone and, even if we did, we couldn't speak English. So we didn't know how to call for help. Our best strategy was to leave the apartment via the fire escape. But they had anticipated our move.

As we were descending down the fire escape, many armed policemen pointed their guns at us. With my very limited knowledge of English, I understood one policeman with a megaphone instruct me not to put my hand in my pockets or they would shoot me on the spot. I was trembling and scared. At the very least, I thought we would end up in jail for nothing we had done.

The gang members tried to turn the police against us. They managed to paint a picture of us as a group of dangerous criminals to them. I don't know what they told them, but the police behaved as if they would have a shoot out with us at any moment. As I descended, they tackled me and threw me against the wall and searched me.

Once they had searched me they began to try to communicate with me. However, I didn't know their language. The gang members, however, were saying all kinds of things that I did not understand.

Things changed for the better when the same business man who had saved us before came to our rescue again. He immediately intervened, and explained to the police that it was the opposite to what the gang had led them to believe. He explained to them that we were Christian youths who never gave anyone any trouble. In contrast, he told them that the accusers were gang members and trouble makers who wished to harm us. The police believed him and quickly turned against the gang and arrested some of them.

After that ugly episode, the word was out on the street, "Leave town or die." That was our only choice. We stayed with some family for the next few days. No more than a few weeks later, a fire broke out in the apartment complex. The smoke moved fast. The building had no fire security system. We ran very quickly out of the apartment. However, as we reached the first floor, I realized that my youngest brother, Daniel, was missing. Without hesitation or fear, I ran quickly back into the building. The building was filled with smoke. With a handkerchief on my face, I ran up several flights of stairs to the third floor.

I looked in the apartment very quickly. I noticed that the fire escape window had been opened. Therefore, I assumed that my brother had used it to get out. As I was descending down the stairs, just about the time that I reached the second floor, I began to lose my breath. It was a very close call. By all accounts, I should have died of smoke inhalation on that day, but God had a better plan for my life.

TIME TO MOVE

We eventually heeded the threats and moved from Trinity
Avenue in that awful neighborhood. If there was a trinity there,
it surely wasn't a holy one. After that initial move, we relocated some five times until we realized that the time had come for
us to consider moving as far away from the Bronx as possible.

Nonetheless, we continued strong in our faith. Shortly after my conversion, my brother Samuel and a childhood friend
named Maxi, accepted Jesus as their LORD and Savior. Maxi
has always been a very methodical person. We admired his intelligence and his rapacious appetite for knowledge.

As we began to consider our move, Maxi became a key
player in our decision making and shaping the strategy for our
relocation. We studied maps, statistics, economy, culture and
the lifestyle of all the states in the United States. After a fair
accumulation of information, we made comparisons and de-
bated the pros and cons of a move to any of these states. And
the winner was—little "Rhody". We decided on Rhode Island
because it was small and presented better opportunities for us.
Once we agreed, a plan was set in motion to visit the State.

Samuel and Maxi became the explorers. They didn't have
much cash then, but were so intrigued about possibilities the
adventure presented that they decided to go anyway. They arrived in downtown Providence in the summer of 1970. Not
having any money for hotels, they slept outdoors in the park,
in front of the largest hotel in the area. The police tried to get
them to move on but somehow they managed to stay. The next
day, they located a Pentecostal church congregation—the only
such church in town. The church members were excited about
their account of how they got there and pledged to provide
transitional housing in their homes until we were able to relo-
cate. I can never forget the love of the members of that congregation as they helped us and went out of their way to make our
relocation as painless as possible.

Once we relocated, we got busy resettling and adjusting to
a new and much different environment. Samuel and our friends

began to work. I continued attending high school. Incidentally, I graduated from high school in 1973 and immediately went on to college. At that point I became detached from church activities due to the demand of college life. However, just as I was about to finish my undergraduate work, I began to feel the need to get involved again. It was a complete reentry. You could say that I was backslidden.

I returned to the church where my father was serving as the pastor. At that time I had began working toward my Master in Education degree at the state college. A few years later, I began to assist my father in various capacities. This was to become my initiation into the ministry. Of course, parallel to this, I also had a community and political life. But the draw into the ministry was so strong that I eventually left education, politics, and secular work to serve my precious LORD and Savior.

CHAPTER 4

The Beginning of Formal Ministry

A CHANGE OF THE GUARD

ittle did I know that the LORD had set me apart to succeed my father in the leadership of the church. At first, I was just delighted to serve as his assistant. But my father felt a call of the LORD to finish a certain business that God told him was left unfinished when he immigrated to the United States. He was to return to the Dominican Republic and continue helping with the expansion of God's kingdom there. It was a gradual process. My father would leave for the Dominican Republic for a month at the time. During his absence, I would assume more responsibilities than usual with a team of leaders in the church.

I remember some of those days were very agonizing. It is one thing to help a pastor, yet another thing altogether to do the job of one. At times, I would be overwhelmed and would beg my father to come back and take over. It was at that time that I convinced myself that I was not cut out to be a pastor— ever! I had too many plans to accomplish for myself and this job was too complicated and difficult.

After a number of trips to the Dominican Republic, my parents sat down with me and broke the news. They had felt distinctively that the LORD was calling me to become the next pastor of the church. In retrospect, I'm sorry to say that I didn't jump for joy upon hearing the news. I remember responding with something like, "Are you sure that it is God's will for me to do something like that?" My parents felt that the instruction from God about this was real and told me to seek the LORD about it. While meditating about this challenge, I considered all I had to leave and questioned how I could do such a difficult job given that I was also employed full time and had a young family. Well, God won! Once I felt it was truly God's call, I made the decision to trust Him on the matter. One thing led to another, and in the summer of 1990, I was elected, by the congregation, and anointed by the presbyter of our denomination, the Assemblies of God, as the new pastor of the Door of Refuge Pentecostal Church. However, that was the beginning of sorrows for me.

RESISTANCE TO CHANGE

Some of the members of the congregation did not accept me as their pastor. I tried to win them over, but to no avail. There were a few, very powerful people in the congregation who did everything they could to undermine my leadership. I was very vulnerable and did not enjoy the additional demands on my time due to the responsibilities in my secular job. It was very evident that I was not respected by them as their new pastor. Most of them eventually left the church.

In fact, the congregation shrunk appreciatively. I began to be very troubled by this chain of events. If God really called me for this job, why was everybody leaving? I started convincing myself that maybe we didn't hear accurately from God after all. Things were not going well.

CHAPTER 5

The Glory of the LORD Fills the Temple

ANOINTED TO SERVE

n desperation, I began to pray fervently. In fact, I asked those who remained from the exodus to pray with me. We turned all the services of the week into prayer meetings for a while. I simply didn't know anything better to do. Nothing seemed to change. One day I woke up in the morning very worried about all this. I decided to go to the church. I was finished, I thought. Who was I kidding? This business of being a pastor was not for me. How pretentious was I to think for a moment that I could do such a difficult and demanding job at that point in my life?

As I entered the church building I headed straight for the altar. I began to cry like a baby. I went down on my knees but had no strength to remain kneeling, so I laid down flat on my belly. I cried out to the LORD. " O, LORD, what have I done? I entered into a job that You have not called me to. I don't feel like You are with me. Look at my anguish and suffering. It seems that my enemies have defeated me. Maybe they were right and I was wrong all along. I have been going against Your will. I need an answer, LORD. I don't want this job if

You have not called me. I need to hear from You, LORD." I was desperate and felt terribly alone.

At that very moment, at the altar, I heard in my mind a command from God. "I want you to separate yourself for three days in fasting and prayer, in this temple. Here, I will speak to you." The moment that I heard His voice, I stood up with a great sense of reverence and expectation. I wiped my tears and walked out of the church that day with clear direction and a renewed sense of purpose.

In the interim between the three day retreat and the time the LORD spoke to me, I felt sort of how an employee feels who has been summoned for a job review. I was a nervous wreck because I expected the worse. Would the LORD confirm my worst fears? Would the LORD rebuke me for having moved into a position I was not called for? Even though I felt such emotions, I was relieved to know that one way or another there was going to be an end to my misery. I couldn't stand the situation any longer.

Shortly thereafter, I spoke with the church leaders about what I'd heard from the LORD. I told them that for three days I would be isolated, alone in the church's office. I was not to be disturbed with any business at all.

The very next week, at the appointed time, I started the retreat on a Monday night. I started praying at about 9:00 p.m. An elder from the church accompanied me until about midnight. After I prayed for several hours, I decided to go into my office where I had a very simple bed.

As soon as I lied down on the mattress, I found myself struggling with a demonic entity. I heard it enter the room and walk towards me. The presence of that demonic being was unnerving. It came closer to me and knelt down beside me. As I tried to turn to confront it, it held both of my arms, pinning them down to the floor. Its strength was certainly superior to mine and it was clear that it came to harm me. As I laid there helpless, I became acutely aware that I needed help. So I invoked the name of Jesus. With great resolve and confidence I said, "I rebuke you in the name of Jesus!" As I used the name of Jesus, the demonic entity suddenly released me and quickly moved away through the office door and kept going out the exterior door.

From that moment on, I felt at peace. However, things were about to get even more interesting. As soon as the demonic entity left the room, I found myself standing in front of a wall. At first, I thought that it was the wall of the office which was near to where I was. However, that was not the case. As I stood in front of the wall, I was curious as to what I would do next. It seemed as if I was being urged to walk through that wall. But how could that be? You don't just walk through walls! Instinctively, however, I extended my right arm to touch the wall. It was as if I was exploring the possibility. As I tried to touch the wall, my hand went clear through it, much to my amazement. As I experienced that, I felt encouraged to walk through the wall to the other side.

On the other side, I found myself inside an unfamiliar but spectacular building. It was very serene and quiet in there. I was in a state of awe as I began to appreciate the splendor of that place. I realized that I was in some kind of worship center. I looked forward and noticed two majestic wooden columns in front of what appeared to be a large altar area. It was not exactly like the altars we are accustomed to seeing in evangelical churches, but it was the same general idea. I noticed that the walls of the temple were very tall, maybe 20 feet high. Everything was finished in precious wood. The workmanship was rich with excellent, hand-carved designs. Among those designs, I noticed many grape vine decorations; all very beautiful and in great detail. I was in profound admiration and wonder at the beauty and splendor of that place. As I looked at the wonderful carvings and designs, I thought to myself, "If the LORD ever allowed me to build a temple for Him, how I would love to duplicate such a beautiful design." As I looked at the decorations at the top of the walls, I noticed movement near the left hand column in front of the altar area.

I quickly turned my attention from the carving details and looked attentively ahead. As I did, I saw the figure of a man dressed in a white robe. He was a person of age and visible wisdom. His hair was white as snow. He came from the left side in front of the altar and proceeded to walk from the left of the altar to the right toward the first massive column. He was walking sideways with His right shoulder towards me and looking forward. As He reached the left column, He briefly disappeared behind it as He continued to move forward. It took Him quite a few seconds before He emerged from one end of the column to the other. When He did, He continued walking very confidently and slowly. My heart was beating fast. My senses were put on high alert. I did not feel fear, per se, but I understood that I was witnessing something very special and highly unusual.

As He made His way toward the second column, I was in a state of amazement. He approached the second column and, as was the case with the first column, it took Him quite a few seconds before emerging on the other side passed the column. To me, it felt like an eternity. I was extremely curious at this point as to whom this majestic person might be. As He emerged from the cover of the column, He walked very slowly. However, this time He stopped and turned toward me. I felt like I was going to faint. As He faced me, His eyes were bright "as fire", looking at me. Without saying one spoken word, He caused me to look up to the ceiling. As I did, I heard a loud noise, greater than the noise of a jumbo jet when it flies low overhead. The noise sounded like a mighty rushing river in a quiet forest.

Then I saw the part of the ceiling where I was standing open; one side to the left, the other to the right. The movement was slow but steady. Suddenly, a cascading, massive, rushing river began to penetrate the opening of the ceiling in the temple and falling downwards in my direction. At that point, I feared for my life. The weight and impact of such a large volume of rushing water would have crushed me. It was a flowing river of crystal clear water that revealed the common whitening of water when it is agitated and full of life. As that river began to descend, I felt my mouth open. I don't think that I intentionally opened my mouth. It was an involuntary movement that I believe was caused by the man who was at the altar of the temple. As my mouth opened, the immensity of the water became closer and closer and faster. However, as the front of the body of water began to approach my face, the river narrowed into the shape of a funnel, narrow enough to fit into my mouth. As the water rushed into my body, I began to lose my strength and remember falling down to the ground on my face. I cried out in a faint voice and said, "O LORD, O LORD, O LORD!"

REVIVAL BREAKS OUT

The impact of the experience that night changed my life dramatically as far as my relationship with the Holy Spirit. As I went to the bathroom to brush my teeth that morning, I was stumbling and out of strength. As I tried to brush my teeth I also noticed my hand was shaking. But I was full of joy and tranquility. For the next few days and weeks I felt like I was walking on clouds. The LORD had certainly spoken to me in a big and impacting way. Furthermore, He didn't rebuke me or confirm my worst fears as I expected! He was loving and kind. He filled me with His Spirit in a powerful and complete way! The joy that radiated from my heart was visible. My trust in God catapulted to new heights. I became certain that God had indeed called me to the ministry. As far as I was concerned, I was personally anointed by Jesus to be His humble servant and minister of His Word. Indeed, I was filled by the awesome Spirit of God. Having been in the presence of Jesus produced a feeling in me that words cannot adequately describe. Plus, I was not afraid anymore. I was not doubtful or uncertain about my calling. Once you look into the eyes of Jesus, you can never be the same!

For the remainder of the next two days of fasting, I didn't experience anything as extraordinary or powerful as the first night. However, I did receive plenty of instruction from the Holy Spirit as I meditated in solemn prayer. During those special moments of quite fellowship with the Holy Spirit, I received instructions pertaining to sin in the church, training the church in spiritual warfare, and our eventual relocation to a better, more spacious building.

To me it was very interesting that such a powerful experience occurred on the first day of my fasting. I feel the LORD wanted me to know that what I experienced was not the result of the stress produced by hunger when you fast. I saw Jesus so calm and serene, as if I was awake. What a wonderful moment that was. From that point on, I made a commitment to follow the guidance of the Holy Spirit at all times. I stopped being so judgmental and stiff in my spiritual life. I decided not to question the Holy Spirit. From then on, I would simply obey the LORD.

The joy of the experience caused me to share with members of the congregation, and especially the leadership of the church, many of the things I had seen and heard. But I didn't do that until my fast was complete. Don't misunderstand me, I have fasted for much longer than that. But God told me specifically to fast for "three days". That was enough for Him to reveal Himself to me in such marvelous way at a time of crisis when I thought that all was lost.

FRESH WORD OF FIRE

I began noticing a change in my preaching. I spoke with boldness and power. Unlike before, people who heard my preaching were attentive. More important, people began to give their lives to Jesus with tears in their eyes. Things began to happen. New people began to come to the church and supernatural things started happening.

For instance, one night while I was preaching, I felt a suffocating feeling in the church. There were many new people listening, but something was wrong. I sensed it in my spirit. I felt impressed to stop the preaching. The LORD revealed to me that there was a demonic presence among the people and instructed me how to deal with it.

I stopped the preaching and told the congregation that the LORD revealed to me that there was a demonic presence in the church. I was instructed to call two deacons to the altar and give them the anointing oil. With the anointing oil, the deacons were to anoint every single person present. As one of the deacons was about to approach one particular person, the demon in that person manifested violently and tried to harm the deacon. As I came down from the altar to assist the deacon, another person who had been sitting in a bench right behind the first demon-possessed person also began to manifest violently. The latter was actually trying to steal money from the purse of the woman in front of her when she fell to the ground. Both individuals were successfully set free from demonic possession on that day by the power of God! Something powerful was happening in our church. The demonic forces were put on a state of alert. Evil spirits could no longer linger or be present in our church. It was like a spiritual eviction notice to the forces of darkness! Indeed, the first phase to the revival in our church was a strong liberation anointing that devils could not resist.

That liberation anointing became an all-out war as the forces of hell were unleashed on our ministry to destroy it. All kinds of demon-possessed people came into our church and attempted to derail the services. Very often our services would turn into liberation services. We were inexperienced and made many mistakes, but we learned as we went along. Many demon-possessed people were being set free by the power of Jesus! Even people who didn't think they could deal with such influences in their lives received deliverance

CHAPTER 6

New Heights in Ministry

RISE UP AND GO

Soon the LORD began to speak to my heart about the need for us to move on. Our church building was relatively small, with a total capacity for about 70 people. It was tiny and we began to feel the need for a larger facility. I had been persistently praying to God for clear direction on this matter. I felt that God had called me to develop a much larger ministry but the space did not match the calling. I began to talk to the leadership about this and a lively debate quickly ensued. Some of the members of the board felt that I should not be thinking about that, given that the present location was not 100% full. They argued that the size of the present congregation could not support a larger building with more overhead.

However, I pointed out that the time had come for us to really take a step of faith. If we waited until all the safety factors were in place to make our move, to me, that would simply mean that we'd be moving according to human expectations and not by faith. God was challenging us to take a gigantic step of faith in the ministry. After much debate and discussion, the day came for a vote. I was not quite sure how things would turn out given the logical and persuasive arguments of the opposite point of view. But the decision was made on the side of faith. On that day, by a majority vote, the board gave me the green light to begin searching for a larger building.

It didn't take too long for us to find a new location. In fact, even the board members that were on my side began to wonder if I was moving too fast. The whole situation was a bit intimidating. We only had $700.00 in the bank. That money was there as a result of an offering that a sister in the church gave for the church to buy a better vehicle for transportation given the fact that our van, which was donated to us by another church, was in very bad condition. I used to joke that our bus was a replica from the Flintstones cartoon, since the floor had rotted in some areas to the point that you could see the street as the bus was moving. We were hoping to multiply that $700.00 through various fundraisers in order to accumulate enough for a better van.

After the board's decision, my wife, Debra (Debbie), and I began immediately searching for a building. One day, as we were traveling down the same street where our church was located, we noticed a large boarded-up building. Curiously enough, the building had been vacant for about four years, but we hadn't noticed it before. Debbie and I entered the parking lot and parked our car facing the building. We looked at each other and sat in the car in awe for about 15 minutes without speaking. Compared to what we had, what a majestic building it was! Debbie interrupted the silence, "Well, what are we waiting for? Let's go claim that building for ourselves!"

We got out of the car and approached the main entrance on the parking side. The doors were boarded up but there were small openings where you could peek into the front lobby area. We were so excited when we saw the wide double doors. We proceeded to lay hands on the building and claimed it as ours in the name of Jesus!

Naturally, and with good reason, many people were wondering where I would find the money to buy the building. Believe me, I preached plenty of sermons about faith and waiting upon God at that time. But even so, the opposition only seemed to grow and get more intense. Some people really thought that I had lost it! But God was always on our side. Given the recent revelations I had from the LORD, I felt that nothing could stop us.

GOD'S FAVOR IN NEGOTIATIONS

The building we found was at one time a very famous Italian restaurant. It had closed down due to changes in demographics. The Italian population that once supported that restaurant began to move into the suburbs in large numbers during the 70's and 80's. At the same time, a large influx of Hispanics made inroads into the city neighborhoods. It just so happens that I have a background in housing. Fresh out of college, I decided to join a very innovative and new community housing organization named SWAP (Stop Wasting Abandoned Property). The community organization evolved out of the need to deal with a high volume of abandoned houses in the city that resulted from the changes in populations. I worked for the organization for three years and, as a result, learned a great deal about the real estate market.

My experience in housing facilitated my search in trying to find the owner. I eventually did locate the owner who had moved to Florida. I called him and told him that I represented a church that was interested in purchasing his building. He was not very enthusiastic since, according to him, he had gone through the process with numerous well-intentioned groups, religious and businesses alike, but nothing ever materialized in terms of a sale. He told me that the only way he would come from Florida back to Rhode Island was if we felt that we were serious and ready enough to buy. I indicated to him that we were ready.

The owner did come to Rhode Island to meet with me at the premises. However, he expressed dismay when he learned that we did not have any money for a deposit. As he was getting back into his car to leave, I begged him to listen to what I had to say. I am not sure how it all happened, but by the time that man left the parking lot of that property, he had made a verbal commitment to sell us the building without any cash deposit. Not only did he finance the deal at a low interest rate, he also was kind enough to accept our church building as a deposit. For almost one year, he allowed us to rent out the other building and keep the rent!

It is worth mentioning here that as this book was being written, the former owner of the property paid me a visit. He came into the building with his son. He said he was in the neighborhood and wanted to stop by and say hello. I took the opportunity to give them a word from the LORD. He was very receptive and expressed great gratitude that I took the time to give him that word.

I also told him that I always talk about how the negotiations with him went when he came from Florida to listen to a young pastor full of faith but with little cash in hand for such a large transaction. He laughed at that and told me that he often jokes about it with his friends too, because they couldn't believe that anyone would do such a thing. I reminded him that what he experienced at that time was the supernatural power of God. He smiled in agreement. You could see that he was very happy to be inside the church building. I took time to explain to him that none of this was a coincidence. He is a man with a good heart, I explained, but good work alone would never translate to access into eternal life. He needed to ask Jesus for forgiveness of his sins and begin a new life as His follower. He listened attentively with a wide smile on his face and once again thanked me for my interest in his salvation. He left the building full of the word of God in his heart.

Two Men of God

The attorney who helped me with the process of purchasing the new building became instrumental in my acquaintance with an evangelist who was known in the area as the "Fisherman from Galilee." He was actually a fisherman before becoming an evangelist and he actually lived in a fishing town by that name—Galilee. I attended one of his revival services at the invitation of my attorney. As I was standing and listening to the worship, I began to cry uncontrollably. I was very embarrassed, so I opened my hands and hid my face in the palms of my hands. I felt broken and naked in my spirit. I could never, in an awakened state, remember having such a feeling. I knew I had come before the presence of God. The Holy Spirit was there in such a real way. As I lost myself in the glory of God, I could not contain myself. Tears flowed from my eyes until I was nothing but a mess.

As I felt I was about to drop to the floor, a gentle hand descend upon my shoulders and a friendly voice asked me, "Do you feel the presence of the Holy Spirit?" I didn't speak a word, but simply nodded my head in agreement without taking my hands off my face to look at the stranger who spoke to me. I later had the opportunity to speak to him and a friendship developed. I later learned his name was Bob Bradberry, better known in the evangelistic circles as the "Fisherman from Galilee."

Bob moved in a strong anointing of the Holy Spirit. I was not accustomed to being around men of God with such supernatural power. I was a bit hesitant to invite him to our church. I was raised under very conservative teaching. At an earlier time, I would have never established a friendship with this kind of an evangelist. But I always remembered the promise I made to the LORD when He visited me. I promised Him that I would never be afraid of the demonstration of the supernatural power of God as I was before. I would trust the Holy Spirit to lead me and the Word of God to be the final judge of such manifestations.

But what would my deacons say after this evangelist visited our church and turned our theology upside down? How would they react to seeing people fall on the floor and others seeing visions? Our people were definitely not used to that. If anything, our deacons were trained to look at such manifestations with a healthy dose of suspicion.

Against all common sense, I decided to invite the evangelist to our church. I knew from that point on things in the church would never be the same. For one thing, I was certain that the small remaining number of people would be further reduced.

Brother Bob came at the appointed time. We had done much preparation in fasting and prayer. I was very apprehensive but sensed in my spirit that I was doing the right thing. When Brother Bob came into the church, the very first thing he did was to meet with me in my office. There he prayed with me and told me that at that moment God would transfer to me an impartation of his very powerful anointing. I was not used to such things, but I dared myself to believe.

He ministered the Word of God with much simplicity and clarity. Then he made an altar call. To my surprise, the two most unlikely people came forward—two of the church deacons. One of them was one of my most ardent critics. She would always say that no one was going to make her fall to the ground. But that night, she was the first to fall on the floor and she laid there for the longest time. I think she was a bit embarrassed when she was able to come around because she couldn't explain what had happened to her.

Bob continued to visit with our congregation. He often mentioned that he felt God had called him to minister among the Hispanic people. It was no wonder that, later in his ministry, he held a revival crusade in Bolivia. What was so unique about Bob's ministry was the fact that he had a special calling to work with children. When he ministered to children, you could listen to the children's account of their visions and experiences with Jesus as they were under the anointing of the Holy Spirit. He became well known nationwide for his special ministry to children.

SPOILS OF WAR

The move to the new location was swift and decisive. What a magnificent building, compared to what we had before! You see, God called us to minister in one of the poorest neighborhoods in the state. Since then, I have had the opportunity to travel around the country and attend services in some very impressive churches. I have seen some magnificent church buildings! When you see these awesome structures sometimes you wonder whether the people appreciate what they have. I also wonder, in some cases, if some of those very blessed congregations have not lost track of the most important things in the ministry. In other words, it seems to me that sometimes churches go beyond the pure desire to build an awesome temple to the glory of God, and get lost in the fleeting vanity of competing with the largest ministry in their immediate area. One also wonders to what extent the leadership of such wealthy ministries are able to escape the danger of pride that often accompanies such efforts. Are we still doing it for God's glory? Or are we building empires to the glory of man?

Most people in our congregation and the Christian community were in disbelief. I remember my father walking into our building and saying, "This is the spoils of war." He knew that we had prayed hard before that victory. The power of God manifested in the new location as well. Also, the strong liberation anointing continued at our new facility. My wife and I, together with the leadership, were becoming exhausted as more and more people would come to the church seeking relief from demonic forces. The anointing for liberation was so strong that strange things began to happen around the perimeters of the church building. For instance, we began to receive threats from satanic groups in the city.

Don't take me wrong, there were many other manifestations of the power of God in our midst, but the deliverance ministry proved very exhausting and emotionally draining. The joy of it all was to see people lives changed. That's what kept us going.

However, in addition to all that, there was a very special and real presence of God in the place. Visions, healings, prophecies, liberations, revelations; it seemed as if God had released all the gifts of the Spirit to function in our midst at once. We spent hours in the awesome presence of God. Also, powerful healings of dreaded diseases such as tuberculosis and cancer were also taking place. We even experienced a resurrection from the dead.

A brother in the church fell to the ground suddenly while I was preaching. A medical doctor who was present rushed to assist him. I also came down from the platform because I perceived the problem to be serious. When I approached the man, the doctor was frantically trying to revive him. His pulse was gone and, for all intents and purposes, he was dead. I got close to his ear and, with a soft voice of authority, I commanded the spirit of death to loosen its grip over him. I gave that command in the powerful name of Jesus. Immediately, the brother opened his eyes and began to breathe again. At the writing of this book, that man still attends our church and so does the doctor.

CHAPTER 7

An Encounter with God

THE STAGE IS SET FOR THE VISION

We moved into the new building in 1995. Once we established ourselves in the new building, it didn't take long for the size of the congregation to explode. Within about one year's time, we grew about three times above the numbers at the former location. Within about two years' time, the congregation had grown six times its size, from about 40 to well over 300 Sunday attendees.

The glory of God descended so powerfully in our midst that the Christian community around us began to notice. People would come in numbers. Every night was an adventure. But we were always certain that God would move mightily among us. People would fall under the anointing for hours. Very often, we would be in church until the early hours of the morning.

It was during those first years, when the anointing of revelation, visions, healing, prophecy and liberation was so strong among us, that God gave me a powerful vision of revival for the United States of America. There was strong commitment to fasting and prayer also in our church. The body of believers has been challenged to walk in the Spirit. In the middle of this powerful anointing, early one morning in the spring of 1998, the LORD spoke to me in another vision. The supernatural demonstration of God's power was so strong that some pastors in the area became critical of us, fearing that their members were transferring to our church. But we kept a firm commitment. As a church growth strategy, we would reach out to the lost and would accept church transfers only after due and careful consideration. To this day, that is still our commitment.

One particular Spanish radio station became very critical of what was going on in our congregation. A particular pastor of the church the radio station was located in blasted us almost daily. People came to me and asked me if I could do anything about it. My response was always that what is of God will remain, and what is not of God will fail.

Indeed, several months into the attacks, the FBI raided that church and confiscated all its communications equipment and computers with arms drawn. It turned out that the radio station was using a frequency from another radio station illegally. Thus the attacks were silenced and the attackers were reprimanded through the court system! That's how the prophetic word came to pass and God vindicated us.

THE BATTLE REACHES HOME

The ministry of liberation became one of our biggest challenges. Ministering to the demonically afflicted sometimes would take us well into the hours of the new day. It became time-consuming and physically and emotionally draining. Every liberation requires individualized attention to the person who has been set free. Counseling sessions lasted for hours.

God is always on time when we need Him. Just about the time we were having all these liberations in our church, a famous Argentinean evangelist named Carlos Anacondia came to a local church to minister. I was asked by the pastor of that church to coordinate the outreach into the Spanish-speaking Christian community. I and some of the leaders in our church were trained by Carlos Anacondia's liberation team in the ministry of deliverance and counseling.

One night, as I was attending an Assemblies of God sectional meeting at a nearby city, I received a beeper message from our home with the urgent 911 number. My wife and I had left our daughters at home and became very preoccupied with the call.

I searched frantically for a telephone at the church we were staying in but could not find one. The pastor of the local church was not at the meeting as of yet. I was very nervous and wanted to go home immediately but felt that it was of the LORD to wait. I looked for a place to pray and pleaded with the LORD to assure me that everything was alright. After feeling reassured, I trusted God about it and waited until the meeting was over.

During our commute, I was very anxious to get home. The call on the beeper was all that my wife and I spoke about during the entire trip. When we finally reached the house, our daughters ran to the door screaming and in a very agitated state. At first, I thought that perhaps a thief had entered the house. They were talking so fast and with such fear that I couldn't understand a word they were saying. While my wife Debra tried to calm them down, I rushed throughout the house looking for an intruder. But I found none.

When I returned to the living-room, my daughters were calmer and were able to explain to us what had happened. It turned out that, while they were watching TV, they began to hear the sound like a roaring lion circling our house. They became very afraid and hid underneath the bed in our bedroom on the first floor. But then, they heard the roaring lion there too. So they ran from the bedroom into the living room and kept close to each other.

In the living room, my older daughter was sitting on the main sofa. Suddenly, she saw the sofa sink down at one end as if someone invisible had sat on it. After the sinking couch incident, they started screaming and ran into another part of the house. By the time we got back home, it seemed as if they had run all over the house out of fear.

I started thinking that perhaps a lion had escaped from the zoo, which was not too far away from us. But that sounded unlikely to me. Surely such a large and loud animal would have been heard by other neighbors. Also, the escape of such a large predator would not have gone unnoticed for very long. But then how do you explain the sinking sofa?

I put two and two together and began to suspect supernatural, demonic activity. Given the nature of the fierce spiritual battles that we were engaged in at the time, it seemed that this explanation would be more likely. Certainly, it could have also been a prank. But, even if it was a prank, it was a cruel and dangerous joke that only an enemy could conceive of.

When we finally went to bed, our daughters were too frightened to sleep alone. I remember not sleeping very well for thinking about the incident. In the morning, I didn't have the energy to go to church. But, given that I had teaching responsibilities, I had no choice. The only thing that was on my mind was the incident. I remember teaching mechanically on that day and hoping that time would go by fast so that I could go back home. I did not feel emotionally fit to deal with church matters that day.

When the service was over, I rushed quickly back to the house. My wife took the girls out so I was left at home alone. I was so distraught that all I could think of was crying. So that's what I did. I cried with a deep feeling of sadness in my spirit. Meanwhile, I was inquiring of the LORD what was happening. I thought that I was fighting the good fight for the Kingdom against the forces of darkness in the name and full support of my Commander in Chief. The demand on my physical body and emotions was difficult at times, but I felt the LORD was with us and we had nothing to fear.

However, when the fight was brought to my door steps and my daughters were targeted, I began to feel vulnerable. Also, questions began to enter my mind as to whether God was watching our rear guard. Had the LORD become displeased with us so that these things were allowed to happen? I felt that if I was being a good soldier on the battlefield, then God would take care of the rest:

> *"But seek first His kingdom and His righteousness, and all these things will be given to you as well. Therefore do not worry about tomorrow, for tomorrow will worry about itself. Each day has enough trouble of its own."*
> (Mt. 6:33-34)

That morning I sat alone on a chair in the living room. I felt alone and defeated. Once again thoughts began to invade my mind. I felt that the LORD would not permit those things if I was doing His will. Maybe I wasn't doing His will in the ministry. So maybe the best thing was to consider quitting the ministry altogether. Those were the kind of thoughts I was having in that difficult situation.

By then, my face was wet with tears. I was crying with my face in my open hands. At that moment, when I was deep in my thoughts, I suddenly heard a knock on the door. I knew it couldn't be my wife or daughters because they never knocked on the door like strangers. I didn't want to get up and answer the door because my face was a mess and I was in no shape to entertain visitors. I was not in a good emotional state at the moment.

But the knocking became too persistent for me to ignore. So I decided to do the best I could to dry my face and approach the door. When I opened the door, there were two men standing there, one of them I vaguely recognized, the other I had never seen before. When the familiar person spoke I recognized him better. He greeted me and introduced the man that was with him.

He said to me that the brother who was with him lived in New Jersey and had never been to Rhode Island before. The distance from New Jersey to Rhode Island is about three and a half hours. Early that same morning, he was awakened by the LORD and given the description of a pastor the LORD wanted him to bring a message to. God described the pastor and indicated the state in which he would find him. The matter was of the utmost urgency and so he traveled to the State of Rhode Island immediately. He didn't waste any time and, after discussing the trip with his wife, he began the journey.

By the time this information was relayed to me, I had already invited both into my house where the discussion continued in my living room. The brother I knew explained that when the brother from New Jersey had reached Rhode Island, he began to inquire in various churches how to find a pastor who met the description he was giving them. He had come to his church that day in search of me.

The brother from New Jersey then spoke. He told me how the LORD had awakened him early in the morning and gave him a burden to find me. He told me that the LORD wanted me to know that He was mindful of my situation. Furthermore, the LORD wanted me to know that He was aware that powerful, demonic forces had risen against me, but that I would be victorious with the help of Jesus. He said I had nothing to worry about!

He also wanted me to know that, when all the spiritual battles had been settled in our favor, the LORD would also deal with my finances. It turned out that I was in a great deal of debt because our income was not sufficient to meet our expenses. The LORD also sent the messenger to inform me, that in the not-too-distant future I would be sitting down with some very powerful people.

I had no question that it was the LORD speaking through him. All the immediate circumstances made that crystal clear to me. We all felt the presence of the Holy Spirit in a very tangible way as we began to praise the LORD and speak in tongues. I praised God and thanked the messenger from New Jersey for his obedience. It took something special to leave his home state to an unfamiliar state and searched for me until he found me. I explained to him how very desperate my situation seemed just a few minutes before, and how I now felt strengthened and empowered by the Holy Ghost!

He said he felt impressed of the LORD to go outside of the house and pray all round it for my home and family. We did that together. When we were done, the man left and I never saw him again. When my wife returned, I told her what had happened and she was filled with the joy of the LORD.

I returned to the ministry emboldened and reassured. The forces of darkness are no match for pastors full of the Holy Spirit! Our victory came to pass. Within months, things began to quiet down. The peace of Jesus permeated the entire church. The Holy Spirit was present in a mighty way in all of our meetings. We were experiencing the kind of supernatural things that can only be described as heaven on earth.

You know that a prophet is true when his word comes to pass. Indeed, within a short period of time later, miraculous things began to happen, fulfilling God's promises. I want to relate a few of them here.

LOSING THE HOUSE

We own a modest home where we have lived since the 1980's. At the time the messenger from New Jersey came to see me, we were in arrears with our mortgage for three months. I was serving as a pastor and working for the state university simultaneously. Still, the income was not enough to cover our expenses. The house was being processed for foreclosure. It was a very sad situation to us because it was a great sacrifice for us to be able to purchase the house to begin with. When I came fresh out of college, I decided to join a local housing community organization by the name of SWAP (Stop Wasting Abandoned Properties). During those years, a large number of dwellings in the city had become abandoned as a result of shifting populations.

The program helped low income residents to purchase these homes at a very modest price, sometimes for as little as one dollar, and to repair it and occupy it. We helped with everything from loan applications to the renovation of the properties. When I left that program after three years with them, I was able to purchase an abandoned home myself and repair it. After living in that home for a number of years, we sold it and invested most of the proceeds into our present home.

Consequently, losing our home meant also losing our hard-earned equity in the house.

We were also continuously hounded by a collection agency that used harassment as a tactic in its collections efforts. We developed a lot of patience in prayer during those difficult days. One day, as I was in my office at the university, my wife called me crying. Of course, I asked her immediately what the problem was. She told me that the bank had sent an inspector to inspect for damages because the house was being placed up for an auction soon and the legal documentation was being finalized on that same day by two o'clock.

I calmed my wife down the best I could and told her not to cry. I felt the enemy wanted to humiliate us and we needed to trust God. I requested permission from work to go home. When I entered the house, my wife was in a somber mood. It was the type of feeling that one experiences when a love one has passed away. We walked to the kitchen silently and sat around the table. The day's mail was sitting on the table.

I told my wife that we had nothing to be anxious about. We would only lose the house if it was God's will. If the LORD was testing us, we needed to remain serene and content with God's decision. As we spoke words of faith, we began to feel at peace. As I was speaking with her, I mechanically picked up a piece of mail off of the table. The letter was from the State Credit Union where I had direct deposit at one time. The university has a few different campuses. I started working at the main campus initially in a suburban area of the state.

However, I wanted to be closer to the ministry in the city, so I requested a transfer. I did that with the objective of switching to pastoral work full time eventually. I was able to use the service of direct deposit on the main campus but not the one in the city. When I used that service, I made a point of having my tithes deducted automatically out of my paycheck and deposited into my savings account. When I left the main campus for the city, I personally went to the credit union and closed down my account there.

I was curious as to why the credit union would be writing to me at all. Perhaps they wanted to inform me of further details related to the closing of the account. But that account had been closed for over one year. When I opened the mail, there was an amount of money included in the report. I remember telling my wife, "You know, when it rains, it pours." I mentioned to her that there was a fairly large amount of money that the bank seemed to be trying to collect from us. But I could not understand why.

The only solution was to call the bank and find out. When I called I was told that the money belonged to me. "But how could it belong to me?" I questioned, given that I closed the account. A lady explained that apparently the bank had made a mistake and continued to subtract 10% of my income and deposited it in a savings account! Since I had already been paying my tithes for the time in question, I could only conclude that it was God's provision. He has many miraculous ways to fulfill His promises.

Right before two o'clock, I rushed to the bank and paid the backed up mortgage payments!

Shortly thereafter, the LORD continued to provide to the point where we became completely debt free except for our mortgage payment. My credit went from very poor to excellent in a matter of a few years. One more time, the LORD was faithful to fulfill His promise! Interestingly enough, God's promises concerning my finances did not come to fruition until I had left my secular job and began to work full time in the ministry.

CHAPTER 8

Visions and Dreams

GOD SPEAKS THROUGH VISIONS AND DREAMS

Then the LORD came down in a pillar of cloud; He stood at the entrance to the Tent and summoned Aaron and Miriam. When both of them stepped forward, He said, "Listen to My words: when a prophet of the LORD is among you, I reveal myself to him in visions, I speak to him in dreams." (Num. 12:5-6)

The reality that the LORD communicates with His people through dreams and visions is evidenced throughout the Holy Scriptures from Genesis to Revelations. To state otherwise is to deny God's word. In fact, these ways of communication from God were to become part of the supernatural experience of every day believer regardless of race, or gender, as long as they were considered children of God. Consider the prophecy of Joel 2:27-29:

"Then you will know that I am in Israel, that I am the LORD your God, and that there is no other; never again will My people be shamed. And afterward, I will pour out My Spirit on all people. Your sons and daughters will prophesy, your old men will dream dreams, your young men will see visions. Even on My servants, both men and women, I will pour out My Spirit in those days."

Some prefer to render a rather narrow interpretation of this promise, perhaps threatened by one of the most outstanding implications in these words; namely, the democratization of the sacerdotal function among the believers as empowered by the indwelling presence of the Holy Spirit. Jesus Himself had to confront an elite, ecclesiastical class who were very used to twisting scriptures to serve their purpose or justify their actions. If it happened during Jesus' time, it should be not difficult to understand why it would be even more so today. In fact, if Jesus were walking in the flesh on the earth today, one can't help wonder about the confrontations that He'd have with many so called "interpreters" of the Scriptures! It is amazing the things we read about and hear these days in the name of Christianity.

> But you are a chosen people, a royal priesthood, a holy nation, a people belonging to God, that you may declare the praises of Him who called you out of darkness into His wonderful light.
>
> Once you were not a people, but now you are the people of God; once you had not received mercy, but now you have received mercy. (1 Pt. 2:9-10)

In the Book of Acts, chapter two, the Word of God reveals what happened on the day of Pentecost. As Peter stood up to boldly explain to the crowds gathered what they just witnessed, he was quick to point out that it was the fulfillment of God's prophecy, given through the lips of the Prophet Joel centuries earlier. This prophecy came to pass as a fulfillment of God's Word, not simply for the generation of the early church, but also for the present generation:

> "The promise is for you and your children and for all who are far off—for all whom the LORD our God will call." (Ac. 2:39)

Peter became one of the New Testament visionaries even though such experiences were not limited to him. In the Book of Acts, chapter ten, the following account is provided:

At Caesarea there was a man named Cornelius, a centurion in what was known as the Italian Regiment. He and all his family were devout and God-fearing; he gave generously to those in need and prayed to God regularly. One day at about three in the afternoon he had a vision. He distinctly saw an angel of God, who came to him and said, "Cornelius!" Cornelius stared at him in fear. "What is it, LORD?" he asked. The angel answered, "Your prayers and gifts to the poor have come up as a memorial offering before God. Now send men to Joppa to bring back a man named Simon who is called Peter. He is staying with Simon the tanner, whose house is by the sea." When the angel who spoke to him had gone, Cornelius called two of his servants and a devout soldier who was one of his attendants. He told them everything that had happened and sent them to Joppa. About noon the following day as they were on their journey and approaching the city, Peter went up on the roof to pray. He became hungry and wanted something to eat, and while the meal was being prepared, he fell into a trance. He saw heaven opened and something like a large sheet being let down to earth by its four corners. It contained all kinds of four-footed animals, as well as reptiles of the earth and birds of the air. Then a voice told him, "Get up, Peter. Kill and eat." (Ac. 10:1-13)

A Gentile and a Jew, according to the New Testament, were having visions from the LORD concerning one of the most important events for the world since the resurrection of Jesus and the outpouring of the Holy Spirit on the day of Pentecost.

As the Scripture develops further, we learn the meaning of God's revelation through this vision to Peter. God was initiating the sharing of the Gospel to the Gentiles. Peter's call in this vision unfolds one of the greatest fulfillments of God's promises. This was a formal outreach into all the nations of God's saving grace through His Son Jesus Christ. In that great plan of salvation, you and I were included.

WHERE THERE IS NO VISION

*Where there is no vision, the people perish: but he that
keepeth the law, happy is he.* (Pr. 29:18 KJV)

When I read this scripture I can't help but remember the
situation that prevailed during the epoch described in the Book
of Judges. Israel had gone astray from her relationship with
God and set her sight on false gods. Their major mistake was
disobedience. God was present with them and led them to victory after victory over their enemies, who possessed the land
of Canaan until Israel conquered and settled it.

But they disobeyed God by not completely driving out
all the inhabitants of the land. The LORD was displeased with
that so much that He asked the people this question:

*"I brought you up out of Egypt and led you into the land
that I swore to give to your forefathers. I said, 'I will never
break My covenant with you, and you shall not make a
covenant with the people of this land, but you shall break
down their altars.' Yet you have disobeyed Me. Why have
you done this?"* (Jdg. 2:1-2)

Israel had not only disobeyed God royally, she actually
was influenced by the pagan worship of those nations to the
point that she began to worship Baal, the chief male deity of
the Canaanite and the Phoenicians. And here is what God had
to say about this:

*"Now therefore I tell you that I will not drive them out
before you; they will be [thorns] in your sides and their
gods will be a snare to you."* (Jdg. 2:3)

With such disloyal behavior, Israel finally managed to
distance itself from God's favor and protection. All throughout
the days of Joshua the people served the LORD. But their worship had been contaminated by the practice of idolatry among
the people. One cannot help but see the remarkable similarity
to our present days of "religious tolerance" and rejection of
God's influence in this society.

However, after Joshua and his generation passed away, a new generation arose that was described as ignorant of God and lacking the historical knowledge of God's previous favor of Israel.

It was at this point that the worst case scenario for Israel began to unravel. The idolatrous practices of the Canaanites and Philistines finally took over as the dominant religion in the land of Israel. Imagine that! The lack of knowledge about God and the mighty things that He'd done for His people throughout generations past was simply discarded for the worship of pagan gods. Sound familiar?

What was God's response to the apostasy of that generation?

In His anger against Israel the LORD handed them over to raiders who plundered them. He sold them to their enemies all around, whom they were no longer able to resist. Whenever Israel went out to fight, the hand of the LORD was against them to defeat them, just as he had sworn to them. They were in great distress. (Jdg. 2:14-15)

The Bible says that God allowed the situation in those days to deteriorate to the point of anarchy:

In those days Israel had no king; everyone did as he saw fit. (Jdg. 17:6)

No Word, No Vision

The boy Samuel ministered before the LORD under Eli. In those days the word of the LORD was rare; there were not many visions. One night Eli, whose eyes were becoming so weak that he could barely see, was lying down in his usual place. (1 Sam. 3:1-2)

Here we find a story that illustrates the severe consequences among the people when God's appointed watchmen develop vision problems. Eli here represents the religious leadership of our time. I am referring here to those God has appointed to be watchmen for righteousness and integrity as examples to the people.

It is interesting and ironic that Eli was losing his natural sight at the same time as his spiritual sight. His priesthood was marked by corruption and scandals. When material things, such as power, and the mundane pleasures of life control the priesthood, the spiritual senses become dull and useless as a way for God to provide direction.

As a result, the word of God becomes scarce. O don't take me wrong! There is indeed a lot of words and platitudes in the name of God, but those words spring from a dried up well of deceit and self-promotion, camouflaged in the form of academic achievements. Before God's eyes, it is what it is—dust in the wind!

I'm not suggesting that this is the condition of entire ecclesiastic leadership in the country. As it was in the case of Eli, there has always been a remnant bravely engaged in the fiercest battle to retain God's heritage. So God raised up a faithful priest in a young boy named Samuel. God's Word became scarce and so did the visions. I do believe here that the Word is speaking about the priesthood as well as the prophet. For the LORD had made it clear earlier that He speaks to prophets in dreams and visions.

How was it possible that one of the greatest prophets of all times was brought up under the direct supervision of a corrupt priest? Notice the urgency of the situation. God began to speak to the future mighty prophet when he was only a boy. The voice of God was not heard by Eli even though he ministered to God in the temple. Once God had foretold the demise of Eli's priesthood and family, next we find the LORD speaking directly to the young man Samuel, rather than the seasoned Eli.

Sometimes, God will speak through the voices of the least expected when those who are expected to speak and live truth relinquish their responsibility. This is especially true at a time of crisis and scarcity of vision. When the head gets corrupted, it places the entire body at risk.

"Dear LORD Jesus, help us in the ministry remain faithful to Your calling, to remain steadfast in our commitment to represent Your Kingdom as men and women who have surrendered their will to Yours. Help us speak Your truth, and do Your will regardless of the circumstances surrounding us. Let us speak boldly and without fear into the ears and hearts of a generation that has been blinded by the god of this world. Help us, O LORD, to remain faithful to Your calling. Help us to live our lives as men and women of integrity and honor for Your name's sake. Amen!"

Have you ever asked yourself why God speaks to people in dreams and visions? Throughout the Bible, visions and dreams have played a significant role as one of the various ways God communicates with man. In Genesis 15:1, the LORD appeared to Abraham in a vision. In the Apostle Paul's vision of the LORD, recorded in Acts 18:9, the LORD spoke words of encouragement to him at night. He was told not to be afraid of the Corinthian Jews who had persecuted him as he proclaimed the Gospel in their synagogue. The book of Revelation is filled with images and symbols that came to John in the forms of dreams and visions! God still uses this method to speak to His people.

CHAPTER 9

A Vision of Revival for America

THE VISION DESCRIBED

In 1998, our church experienced the beginning of a strong revival. The sick were being healed, the demon-possessed were being liberated, the lost were being saved, and the believers were being sanctified. During the month of May in 1998, I went to bed as usual. However, what happened that night was very unusual. Early the next morning, a revelation from the LORD came to me. It was a very impacting experience. In that vision, I found myself standing in an open area outside. There were no buildings, or any other structures in sight. In front of me, high up in the sky, there was a gigantic map of the United States. Only the outline of the map was visible. It looked as if the definition was drawn in midair without any background but the sky itself. As I looked carefully at the phenomenon, I heard a voice say, "A very powerful fire has started in the northern part of the United States, a fire so powerful that nothing can contain it—and is expected to move rapidly over the entire land." As I listened to the voice and looked at the map, I saw a flame of fire erupt in the northern center area of the United States. Immediately after that fire sprung up, a second flame erupted in the same manner to the right of the first, but in the same immediate area of the map. Soon after the second flame sprang up, the entire map of the United States from left to right, beginning in the north, began to be filled with a light. The light was a bright violet or light purple color. As this color filled the map, many bright white points of light began to appear, until the whole map was filled with the bright violet color and the points of light.

Immediately after the map was filled, I found myself in another location, but still outside. Again, there were no buildings of any kind in sight. The sky was covered with smoke-like clouds. Suddenly, and without warning, an incredible bolt of lightning exploded from inside the clouds and hit the ground. The light produced by the explosion was blinding and astonishing. I had to close my eyes because of the blinding effect of the illumination. The experience was so vivid that I was awakened. I jumped from my bed and fell on my knees, frightened by the experience and what it might represent. I asked God to help me understand what I had seen.

God's answer was immediate, for when I went back into bed, the vision continued. This time, I found myself in the parking lot of the church I pastor. My purpose in going to the church was to communicate to the brethren what I had seen in the vision. I entered the sanctuary and noticed that there was a small group of people sitting near the altar and a brother, who is presently a deacon, was speaking to them. I approached them and waited politely, but very excitedly, for the brother to finish. When he did, I told them about the vision I just had and how I felt that it was a way for the Holy Spirit to alert us to a very powerful revival that was coming to the United States.

After that, I found myself in a different sequence of the vision where I was traveling on a highway. When I came to the end of that highway, I stopped the car because there was no more road to continue on. The highway ended there with a section under an overpass that served as shelter for the homeless. There were about six or seven of them and one was keeping vigil. The others were trying to sleep with sheets of cardboard over them. I approached the man who was guarding the entrance and told him why I was there. I told them that I had come to warn them of a powerful fire that was moving in all directions from the north and it was about to reach here. They needed to be prepared; was the message. That man considered this to be important because he took me to his friends who, at first reacted suspiciously about me, but decided to listen.

When I woke up the next morning, I was very excited and agitated. I began to search frantically for a map of the United States because the whole thing was so clear and I knew exactly the area where the fire went up. Much to my dismay, I couldn't find a map. So I got out of the house and went to find a *USA Today* newspaper, for I had remembered that the publication displayed a weather map of the United Sates on the back. I found a paper box with the last copy of the paper in the window from the previous day. Much to my surprise, the map in the paper only displayed cities and not the name of the states.

I had to wait until I got to my office at the university where I worked. There I finally found a map on the computer with all the information I was searching for. I immediately looked at the area where the fire started and I found that the three states in the north were in the general area of North and South Dakota and Minnesota. The first flame of fire was to the left in the North/South Dakota area and the second fire was to the right in the Minnesota area. I was elated to have identified these states.

Next, I began to ask myself the question, why would the LORD allow me to see that vision? Was this information for private or public consumption? The answer would only be revealed through prayer and fasting. So I started fasting and praying. At work, instead of going for my lunch hour, I would close myself in my office and pray for an answer from the Holy Spirit. I did that for about two weeks. After more than a week in fasting and prayer, the answer came. I was to contact churches in the area in question and tell them about the vision. So I began the process, through the Internet, of identifying churches in the area. I looked for churches that were hungry for revival or that were already experiencing revival.

I began with North Dakota. I located a church there and
spoke with the pastor. The pastor in question had been hungry
for revival but had become disillusioned because of lack of
results. He told me that something happened in his church but
it quickly dissipated. I told him that that was about to change.
God was going to move in a mighty way in that area. I told
him to get prepared. He was kind of skeptical and took my
name and telephone number down anyway. As far as I was
concerned, however, it was not my job to convince anyone.
My job was to relay a message. That was my responsibility;
that was my mission. I told him that the word to him was not
for private consumption and that he needed to contact other
pastors and tell them about it as well and communicate to the
body of Christ what was about to happen.

I then focused on Minnesota. On the Internet, I came
across a church in Alexandria called House of Prayer. I con-
tacted the pastor there and told her about the vision. As we
spoke, we felt the anointing and power of the Holy Spirit in a
mighty way. She told me that the church had been praying for
a sign from God. She felt that this was it. She told me that she
would bring the information to an intercessory group for direction from the Holy Spirit. The very next morning, she called
me and told me that after due prayer, the intercessory group got
word that this was indeed of God! I told her it appeared that
my responsibility had been discharged. I also told her that the
information was not for any particular church but for all that
would hear. She put me in touch with a church in Hutchinson,
by the name of Riverside Assemblies of God. I called the pastor who was also very open to the message and he put it to
prayer with his team of intercessors. The very next day he also
called me and said that his intercessory group prayed and received direction from the Holy Spirit that this was of God!

Next, I was invited to come to Minnesota to relate the
vision personally. I felt honored to go to the land where I saw
the fire. Just stepping on that ground to me was very special. I prayed to the LORD about that trip and got word that
somehow the Mississippi River played a symbolic role in the

impending revival. So I wanted to go to the headwaters of the Mississippi—a place of beginnings. We did go to the headwaters and held a service there.

The LORD gave me a prophetic word about restoration, cleansing, and unity of the body of Christ. It was symbolized by throwing a small tree into the waters of the Lake Itasca, where the Mississippi begins. It was a symbolic gesture of the sweetening and cleansing of the spiritual life of the church body in the United States. Next, we held hands across the river since the Mississippi, which later turns into a raging river, has a very humble beginning. You can actually cross it on foot.

I visited Minnesota on June 19th, 1998, and related the vision to an overflowing attendance in the House of Prayer in Alexandria. The Holy Spirit moved powerfully. Next, we went to Hutchinson where I preached the Sunday service of that weekend. There were many brothers and sisters there, pastors and other ministries represented too. The attendance was overflowing. There were brethren from different states as well.

All this was very humbling to me and I praised the LORD for entrusting such a powerful message to a virtually unknown person like myself and one who is not worthy of such honor. To Him always be the glory and honor forever. Amen!

CHAPTER 10

A Search for Meaning

A CLARIFICATION

At this point I feel the need to provide a little clarification. In the vision of revival for America that I received from the LORD, there is a great deal of symbolism. If I told you that I understood all the symbolic implications, it would be misleading. However, one important thing became very clear to me and that is, the vision had to do with revival in America. How do I know? As is related in the narrative of this vision, I cried out to the LORD to understand its meanings, and He graciously revealed it to me.

Most of my work in the ministry has been based on my calling by the LORD to be a pastor. But the LORD has also spoken to me in dreams and visions. The two most powerful ones you have just read in this book. In the first vision, I experienced the infilling of the Holy Spirit by our LORD Jesus Christ. It was a powerful, unforgettable experience! It radically changed my life! The second vision, which God showed to me, was about revival in America.

The point I am trying to make is that I didn't immediately understand the powerful symbols included in this vivid vision. In other words, the LORD did not take me step-by-step like in the case of Zechariah, Chapter 4. In that passage, the LORD gave him the vision of the lampstand and the two olive trees. It seems to me that the vision was not given to me alone. It was given to the body of Christ to discern the specific meaning of each one of these symbols.

I was favored by the LORD to travel in the area where I saw in the vision and released it. Furthermore, I meditated on it often, and pondered the meaning of each one of these symbols. It was something that I didn't ask the LORD about while receiving it. As a result, I formed my own impression of the meanings. However, such impressions were based on my own discernment as I inquired of the Holy Spirit. I'm sure that others have inquired of the LORD just as I have about these matters and they have received fresh insight.

In my travels to Minnesota and North Dakota, I have received many suggestions and questions as the body of Christ continues to ponder on the various symbols in the vision. The important thing to remember is that the LORD provided the most vital and central part of the message—Revival!

As I provide my impressions of these symbols, I stand in humility completely open to correction and/or corroboration from the larger body of Christ on my interpretation of the symbols in the vision of revival. It wasn't just given to me, but to the church in America as a whole.

THE MAP SUSPENDED IN MID AIR

"In front, high up in the sky, there was a gigantic map of the United States. Only the outline of the map was visible and it looked as if the definition was drawn in midair without any background but the sky itself."

The definitions of the map were very clear. I don't remember any other territory besides the United States included. It was very clear to me that the LORD was speaking of the United States. Why was the map in midair instead of on the ground? Why not hanging on a wall as we are accustomed to seeing maps? Why not even on a terrestrial globe of the world for that matter? The fact that it was suspended in the air indicates to me that God gave this message specifically for America alone. Second, to me this also means that the situation that prevails in the United States is very much in His sight and also that this country is lifted up in the presence of our LORD and Savior. Praise God Almighty! As I focused my eyes on the impression of the map in midair, I don't remember anything else around it. There was not any type of distraction. I had no interest in looking any other way; I was captivated by the vision of the map suspended in midair.

A Voice from Nowhere

"As I was contemplating the vision of the map, I heard a voice from behind me that said: A very powerful fire has started in the northern part of the United States. A fire so powerful, that nothing can contain it, and is expected to move rather quickly over the entire land."

Without any doubt, by now the reader has concluded that the church I pastor is primarily Spanish speaking. Of course, I could have pastored an English speaking church. I came to the United States when I was only 16 years old. So most of my education all the way to graduate school occurred in the U.S. Add to this the fact that my wife is a native born Rhode Islander of Irish descent. In my family, the main language spoken is English. But the church I pastor is primarily Spanish speaking. The minority of English speaking members are assisted by a bilingual interpreter. When there is a reasonable number of listeners present who do not speak English, then we have an interpreter from the front.

When I tried to find a church fresh out of college, I dismissed the idea of coming to church where my father pastored for one major reason; my wife and children were not very fluent in the Spanish language. But, after a long search, I concluded that the LORD was calling me to serve next to my father. So I obeyed even though my wife and I were not in complete agreement about it at first. I felt I had to follow the LORD's leadership on this issue. Thanks be to God, He made the impossible happened. Against all odds, my wife came to Christ, and she became a powerful partner with me in the ministry!

When I think about the voice that spoke in the vision, I remember the English language was used. Given that Spanish is my primary language, I felt the fact that English was used to announce the message was important. It was important because it provides clear evidence that the message was indeed for the United States. First, I saw the very well defined map of the United States, then I heard the voice in English, and then I saw the flames of fire igniting on a very specific location of the U.S. map. In addition, I was blessed to be able to travel to that land. You see now how I arrived at such a conclusion.

I only heard that one audible statement in the entire sequence of the vision. You can appreciate how eager I was to understand it immediately! Was the United States about to be engulfed in some kind of fiery conflict? I immediately developed a sense of urgency. I remember my reaction in the vision as I heard these words. I realized that I was one of a few people to be given a special knowledge with serious implications for America. But I wasn't sure if it was adverse or beneficial. Then the vision continued.

FLAMES OF FIRE

"As I was listening to the voice and looking at the map, I saw a flame of fire erupt in the northern center area of the United States. Immediately after that fire sprung up, a second flame of fire erupted in the same manner to the right of the first, but in the same immediate area of the map."

I never took my sight off the map. Even as the voice sounded from behind, I kept attentively looking at the map. It was as if I knew that something else was going to happen. Indeed, it did. When the voice finished making the statement, I saw a burst of fire spring up in a north central area of the map. The fire was very bright and went up as a flame of fire. I will never forget it. But no sooner than the flame rose up, a second flame of fire to the right sprang up as well in a similar fashion.

At that time I was not certain if that was a fire of judgment or of blessing from the LORD. With the revelation provided later in the vision, that eventually became clear. The fire is symbolic of the Holy Spirit, without whom there can be no revival (Acts 2:3). Are we to understand the two flames of fire as a revival of a double portion anointing?

After reviewing the map of the United States, and noticing that those fires erupted next to each other, I became convinced that the geographical evidence pointed to two adjacent states—Minnesota and North Dakota and their surrounding areas. I didn't see any boundary lines of any states. But, as I looked to the area in question, I found that those states were included, not discounting the possibility of other connecting states. Once again, the fire covered the immediate area in the north central portion of the United States.

THE GLORY OF THE LORD FILLS THE NATION

"...The entire map of the United States from left to right, beginning in the north, began to be filled with a light and bright violet or light purple color. As this color was filling the map, many bright white points of light began to appear. As long as the color was filling the map, the points of bright lights were also appearing until the whole map was filled with the bright violet color and the points of light." Praise God!

It is important to observe that, after the fires appeared, a bright violet or purple color began to fill the entire map from north to south, east and west. This has led me to conclude that the church in that area would be used by God to spread the fire across the land. For so many years I have heard well-intentioned believers boast, with a certain degree of pride, that their states or regions would be keys to revival in America. As far as I understand it, it will flow from the north down in different directions until the entire land has experienced it. Praise the LORD!

The only way this can be interpreted is to say that the glorious bright violet or purple color filling the U.S.A. is the glory of our majestic King of Kings and LORD of LORDs! Such colors were used in the very unique robes of kings in ancient times. Purple is the color of royalty.

> *"They put a purple robe on Him, then twisted together a crown of thorns and set it on Him. And they began to call out to Him, 'Hail, king of the Jews!'"* (Mk. 15:17-18)

I have concluded that the glory of the LORD will fill the land. And as this happens, the presence and radiance of the King will make His church (points of light) shine brighter than ever in the middle of the emptiness and darkness!

> *"I am the light of the world."* (Jn. 9:5)

> *"You are the light of the world. A city on a hill cannot be hidden."* (Mt. 5:14)

POINTS OF LIGHTS

> *"As this color was filling the map, many bright white points of light began to appear. As long as the color was filling the map, the points of bright lights were also appearing until the whole map was filled with the bright violet color and the points of light."*

What do these points of light represent? Do they represent the many houses of prayer that will be illuminated to radiate the King's light as the Glory of God sweeps the land? Or the light that has been hidden under the bowl (Mt. 5:15), being recovered and placed up high where it was destined to be like a light in the middle of darkness? Could these points of light perhaps represent the many prayer and intercessory groups that would come to life at the thunderous voice of the LORD's command? Or, do they represent individual believers set on fire by a double anointing of the power of God? Or is it, all of the above?

I do believe strongly that as the Glory of the LORD fills this land, many will be set ablaze. Indeed, many are already so. Many will have the burning burden of intercession for this nation. The passion and urgency for prayer and intercession is overtaking America at this very moment! Praise God!

Shortly after I travelled to Minnesota and North Dakota, I decided to keep a watch for any signs coming from that blessed area of God. One day, as I was searching for such signs on the internet, I came across a web page that caught my attention. A new and very passionate prayer group has been birthed in the U.S.A. I was intrigued to find out who they were and where it was based. I was very excited! At that point it did not matter where it was based. Just to learn about such a dedicated group in the U.S.A. was enough to send currents of joy and expectation running up my spine. But I did ask myself the question, as I plunged myself deeper into the information, what if such a group came from the area I saw in the vision?

I almost fell off my chair when I learned that the group was based in Minnesota! The goal of the group is to reach every citizen of the United States through the establishment of prayer groups in the homes of believers and churches. It was a highly organized operation using the zip code of the United States postal system. Even more amazing was the staggering numbers of affiliate churches and groups that had already joined the effort at the time. The name of the ministry, appropriately, is *"The Lighthouse Movement."*

I became so excited that I joined our church right away and began to pray for every citizen in the State of Rhode Island. Rhode Island, being a state with many miles along its coast, is home to many lighthouses at points along the shore and beyond. Of course, you can also find plenty of lighthouse souvenirs across the state. I purchased some replicas of lighthouses for my office and for gifts for invited guests and church members. Our people knew how passionate I felt about this so they gave me lighthouse paintings and replicas as gifts for my birthday or Pastor's Appreciation Day!

Sometime later, as my wife was watching Pat Robertson on TV, she called me to hurry into the living room. Rev. Pat Robertson was in front of a map of the U.S. He was explaining something and on the map there were many colored thumb tacks that had been pinned on different areas of the map. As he spoke with an urgent voice, I realized that he was challenging America to pray. He was motivating commitment from different regions and the map was filling up quickly. We decided to follow up with the progress over the next several days. As far as I can remember, he was able to cover the entire map with prayer by believers who called in to stand in the gap. Praise God!

There is an important, additional point to be made here. There is a great lesson to be learned about the appearance of the Messiah in ancient times in Israel. The overwhelming majority of the generation that waited for His coming had the wrong idea. They expected a literal Savior to take up weapons and command an army to overthrow the oppressive and hated regime of the Roman Empire. It was not to happen that way. Instead, the Messiah came as "the Lamb of God!" *"For My thoughts are not your thoughts, neither are your ways My ways, declares the LORD."* (Is. 55:8) As I have seen God's strategy develop with what He is doing, I also see a parallel here.

You see, during the experience of the most recent move of God in America, we basked under the sun of the anointing. Who could blame us? Once you experience God's glory, it becomes an addictive, unending pursuit. You just cannot experience anything like that in the natural! No wonder there are people around called the "God Chasers!" So, we have become so intoxicated with His anointing that we forgot its purpose. God's bottom line is that souls are saved! But something else happened. We adopted a misguided yardstick by which to detect and measure revival.

How does most revival begin? They begin with our eyes being open to our spiritual condition. That produces supplication and prayer, first for our sins, which translates into repentance. The spiritual man is awaken and restored to his right status before God. What occurs once we have been awakened to our decaying condition? The outward manifestations of God's presence are what many often call revival. In fact, the revival has already taken place in the inner man of the believer. The same thing happens even with the nonbeliever that comes to Christ. They are found dead in their spirit and their eyes are opened to their condition by the power of the Word of God and the conviction of the Holy Spirit. Subsequently, they begin to experience the wonderful things of the Spirit life that become manifested in the form of supernatural phenomena.

Here is my point. Many have been looking to signs of God's revelation of a powerful revival in America with the wrong understanding. They have been looking for the fruit (the evidence) and not for what must happen prior to that. It is more exciting to many people to chase after the anointing that occurs after true revival has manifested, than for the signs that must precede it. Nonetheless, God's promise is coming to pass in front of our very own eyes!

CHAPTER 11

The Vision and Recent Events

SEPTEMBER 11, 2001

U nder such new light, it might become easier to appreciate recent events in America as related to God's sovereign move in this nation. Two years before the attack against the twin towers, my wife and I travelled to Minnesota to be part of the initiation of an intercessory effort for America! A particular brother from there began a trip from the source of the Mississippi River all the way to Louisiana in a small motor boat. His name was Jim Hanna. His mission was to intercede for America! I had the privilege of praying in the boat over the first 15 miles of the journey. Exactly two years later, on September 11, 2001, at the same time in the morning, the United States suffered that horrendous attack on its own soil.

That is the reason why I believe that all these major events in America during the past 10 years are not coincidental. Now, I know that there are many people who wonder how God would allow such a thing to happen. Well, it happened! Certainly, I do not refer to such an incident without feeling for the families and those who lost their lives. That traumatic incident left a deep psychological scar we all share in our common psyche. It is very difficult to accept the notion that God would be even remotely related to something like that.

The truth of the matter is that more difficult days await the earth as we move closer and closer to the end times according to the Bible. Many try to sugar coat it and smooth it over to fit the thinking of the times, but God's Word will prevail.

Attacks on America, economic woes, the disintegration of the nuclear family, the erasing of the boundaries of our Bible-based, moral value system, all prove that America needs to turn to God! Not for a week or two, as occurred shortly after the attack. We must truly repent and ask for God's forgiveness as a nation and turn from our ways at all costs. For, if we as a nation persist in our sin, things are only bound to get worse.

The difficult issues that confront this nation might be looked upon as a hard way for God to draw us toward repentance. But it has never been easy for God to turn the heart of a people He loves toward Himself, especially when they have replaced Him with the illusory and deadly pleasures of materialistic idolatry, coupled with the dangers inherent in intellectual pride!

SMOKE CLOUDS, THUNDER AND LIGHTNING

"Immediately after the map had been filled, I found myself in another location, but still in the outdoors. Again, there were no buildings of any kind. The sky was covered with smoke-like clouds."

During the Spring of 1998, I had the honor to visit Minnesota. I later had the privilege to visit North Dakota as well. I could not believe my eyes as I traversed the area by land. It was astonishingly similar to the scenery I witnessed in the vision!

I had been invited to a prophetic conference in North Dakota. As I was traveling further to the northern part of the state, I could not keep silent. I couldn't help but mention to the minister who was taking me to his church to speak, how amazingly similar the scenery was to the place I saw in the vision. There was not a tree in sight, or any structure for that matter!

It was in such an open area that the third sequence of the vision took place. Again, I found myself standing. Having been brought there, I didn't know where I was. I was outside, but I had no sense of orientation because there were no landmarks at all.

It looked as if the events were occurring on a very cloudy day. A very dark cloud was visible. I looked attentively at that cloud just as I looked at the previous scenarios with the map. Of course, the map was no longer present. It was indeed a very surreal experience!

As I waited, without warning, an extremely loud explosion occurred from within the dark cloud. A very powerful bolt of lightning followed. The lightning struck the ground forcefully. The flashing of the lightning was blinding. The noise of the explosion, combined with the strong flashing of the lightning, was too much for me. I woke up in a very agitated state.

Clouds in the Bible can be interpreted in different ways depending on the message. Concerning the LORD's presence, the Bible says:

> *And the priests could not perform their service because of the cloud, for the glory of the LORD filled His temple. Then Solomon said, "The LORD has said that He would dwell in a dark cloud...."* (1 Kgs. 8:11-12)

The glory of the LORD appeared in the temple in the form of a thick, dark cloud which is described by King Salomon in this Scripture. What an awesome sight to behold! The priests could not continue to perform their priestly duties on that glorious occasion because of the awesome presence of the glory of God. I couldn't say that I was very close to that presence, but even so, it was still overwhelming. When that blinding and deafening bolt of lightning exploded out of the cloud, it was all I could stand!

In Exodus 19, at Mount Sinai, God instructed Moses to tell the people to prepare for an encounter with Him where He would speak to the people. For three days they purified themselves. At the appointed time, the Bible describes what happened:

> On the morning of the third day there was thunder and lightning, a thick cloud appeared on the mountain, and a very loud trumpet blast was heard. All the people in the camp trembled with fear. Moses led them out of the camp to meet God, and they stood at the foot of the mountain. All of Mount Sinai was covered with smoke, because the LORD had come down on it in fire. The smoke went up like the smoke of a furnace, and all the people trembled violently. The sound of the trumpet became louder and louder. Moses spoke and God answered him with thunder. (Ex. 19:16-19 TEV) Praise the LORD!

My experience was very similar to the one described above. The obvious difference being that Moses was awake. I was in a dream/vision state. The impact became overwhelming with the sound and sight of the bolt of lightning striking the surface of the earth in front of me, at a distance. The profound joy and exhilaration that I feel as I recount this experience is almost indescribable.

THE ANSWER FROM WITHIN THE VISION

> "In that part of the vision I found myself walking into the church that my wife and I pastor. A group of sisters were sitting at the altar and a brother from our church, a deacon, was talking to them. I approached and informed them of the vision I had and how that meant that a powerful revival like no other was going to come to America. I was very excited as I told them about it."

This is the primary reason why I have been so certain that the central meaning of the entire vision had to do with revival in the U.S.A. I did not understand that clearly until I explained the vision in our church. Of course, the first place where I released the vision was to our own congregation!

I have had the experience of meeting so many men and women of God as I visited the area where I saw the fire numerous times. I have also received many suggestions and possible interpretations of the different symbolisms in the vision.

One particular brother, whom I never got to meet, sent me a message through a friend of his whom I had met. He asked if it was possible that God was also speaking of judgment for America as a way He would bring about revival. My answer to that question was that I was not sure for the mere reason that I did not hear anything to indicate an impending judgment as being the central part of the message. I did find myself explaining to the members of our congregation what the vision was about. It was about revival. There is no question in my mind, however, that time and time again, the Word of God shows that, when the people of Israel fell from the grace of God, sooner or later calamity would follow. In the middle of their suffering, when they had fallen so low that the only place to look was up, that is exactly what they did. They looked up to God for forgiveness and restoration.

Message after message from God to America has carried an urgent tone for repentance, only to fall on deaf ears. In fact, the collective response within the secular world has been to diminish the influence of anything that represents God in the public arena. From the elimination of prayers in schools, to the removal of the Ten Commandments in the court room, American secular culture seems to suddenly be at war with God. And this is not just happening in the secular sector. Many religious educational institutions as well as the denominations that they represent are aligning forces with public opinion in the name of the separation of church and state.

In our own state, I had the opportunity to participate in public hearings where testimonies where being heard from both sides of the same sex marriage issue. The saddest thing I beheld in that hearing was how men of the collar (clergy members) showed up to testify in favor of passing such a bill in the state. These were men and woman backed up by educational attainments and higher education degrees conferred upon them by some of the leading theological institutions in the area.

Suddenly, the godly perspective on this and other crucial issues of our times is being made to appear as intolerant, old fashioned, and obsolete. This is in a state where polls show that a majority of the people oppose same sex marriage. Fortunately, the bill did not pass this time. Instead, a compromise was reached as the pro-gay marriage forces agreed that there was not enough support within the General Assembly this year to accomplish what they have already succeeded with in so many other northeastern states. For now, they would have to settle for a language that recognizes civil unions. You can be sure they are not happy with such an outcome. They have been chipping away at public opinion and have been gradually gaining ground. Next year, they expect, their dream in Rhode Island will become a reality.

In other words, we can certainly understand why many in the body of Christ might feel that America has been dangerously flirting with divine judgment for some time now. It seems the voice of reason has been silenced among many in the church who seek to promote and advance their own corrupted agendas. The point being that, if the LORD has already made this clear through prophetic voices of our times, it is not difficult to understand why such specific warnings were not explicitly included here.

SPREADING THE WORD

> *"After that, I found myself in a different sequence of the vision where I was traveling on a highway and came to the end of that highway. I stopped the car because the road ended. The highway abruptly ended there at a section under an overpass that served as shelter for the homeless. There were about six or seven of them and one was keeping vigil...."*

Who were these men? And why were they at a dead-end, living as homeless people under cardboard shelters? I have asked myself these and many other questions regarding this part of the vision. Has the plight of the less fortunate in

America reached a point where God can no longer remain silent? Is God calling us to action and into account on this?

On the other hand, could the scenario presented here be related to the condition of a great part of the body of Christ, the church, in our midst today? It seems to be at a dead-end, by the side of the road, fenced in and fearful, guarded and protected. In other words, it is irrelevant and incapable of any longer positively influencing our culture from the perspective of God's will and holiness. It is on the defensive against the forces of darkness that seem to be very much on the offensive.

I felt that sense of discouragement from a minister in North Dakota as I released the vision to him. I also felt the fear among some pastors and leaders as they heard the content of this vision. They had a sense of cynicism, protectionism and suspicion. That is not to say that there were not many who were receptive as well.

Consider even a third possible scenario. Could this represent the actual state of affairs in the United States at large? We are financially strapped with our economy reduced to almost recession status, begging for loans to remain afloat, at a dead end, almost at the brink of disaster, and in dire need for a miracle from above?

The truth of the matter is that all three scenarios are very real today! But the one about the church impacts me the most, for we are supposed to be the salt and light of the world. In a sense, we are also to the world as the eye is to the body. If your eye is good, the entire body will be good. (See Luke 11:34.) This nation has been so blessed by God because of a faithful remnant that has shined to the body through generations. I think that many of us agree that something has been missing in the church!

Many have tried to fill the void with attractive programs and sleek marketing campaigns not so different from the way it is done in corporate America. There is an old saying for that which goes something like this: "If you can't beat them, join them!" Indeed, many churches today operate like the American corporation. They have a powerful board of directors, a powerful CEO and a good budget for Research & Development. The main objective becomes to be better than anyone else! Numbers are equated with success, while we move from one scandal to the next. The numbers of moral casualties by now look more like the valley of the dried bones described in the Book of Ezekiel, chapter 37. The strangest thing, however, is that the secular public today responds with a great deal of sympathy and "understanding" at the sight of such deviance in Christian leadership. A high degree of tolerance for moral failure has become the norm in this society, while the call for reform and alignment with God's Word that is made by the remnant in the church is met with scorn and ridicule. Hypocritically, and with a high degree of frequency, that same secular public will use such occurrences among our leadership to point out that we are no different than them. Often they paint a picture of the true remnant in the church as insensitive, intolerant, and out of touch with the times when they call for repentance. The church is indeed becoming like the world!

What is the void that we feel in the church of Jesus Christ today? It is the void left when the mighty working wonders of the Holy Spirit stopped in our services and activities. It was left when the dove was locked up in the cage; silent and grieved, replaced with human ingenuity and a reliance on government funded programming.

The church has become program rich and spiritually poor. Church leadership vies for influence with government funding and services. They wait in line for the scraps that fall from the tables of government and private foundations in order to fill the gap left when the signs and wonders stopped working on behalf of the lost. What a pathetic picture of many churches today!

The modern church can be best illustrated by the church of Laodicea, the rich church which is alluded to in the Book of Revelation:

> "To the angel of the church in Laodicea write: These are the words of the Amen, the faithful and true witness,

the ruler of God's creation. I know your deeds, that you are neither cold nor hot. I wish you were either one or the other! So, because you are lukewarm—neither hot nor cold—I am about to spit you out of my mouth. You say, 'I am rich; I have acquired wealth and do not need a thing.' But you do not realize that you are wretched, pitiful, poor, blind and naked. I counsel you to buy from Me gold refined in the fire, so you can become rich; and white clothes to wear, so you can cover your shameful nakedness; and salve to put on your eyes, so you can see. Those whom I love I rebuke and discipline. So be earnest, and repent. Here I am! I stand at the door and knock. If anyone hears My voice and opens the door, I will come in and eat with him, and he with Me. To him who overcomes, I will give the right to sit with Me on My throne, just as I overcame and sat down with My Father on His throne. He who has an ear, let him hear what the Spirit says to the churches." (Rev. 3:14-22)

I know these are strong words, but they were spoken by the LORD Himself. Before revival comes in earnest, there have to be certain conditions present. There has to be first, a time of brokenness that can only come through humility. Second, there has to be a period of intense prayer and seeking out after God. Third, there has to be a period of repentance. In the Book of Second Chronicles the LORD says it this way:

"...If my people, who are called by My name, will humble themselves and pray and seek My face and turn from their wicked ways, then will I hear from heaven and will forgive their sin and will heal their land." (2 Chr. 7:14)

CHAPTER 12

To Those Who Want to Hear

HUMILITY

You save those who are humble, but you humble those who are proud. (2 Sam. 22:28 TEV)

Why is humility so important to revival? The opposite of humility is pride. This is a condition that can be viewed as a barrier to revival. There has been so much emphasis placed on knowledge lately and the rationalization of our faith. The Bible says that knowledge, though good, can also puff up. This condition is very much present in the Christian community these days. You have to have this degree or that degree in order to be accepted as having authority. Everything has to be put to the test of rational thought. Consider this for a moment, if Jesus would have placed such a disproportionate value on knowledge, as is the case today, He would have selected a very different evangelistic team. Instead of the disciples He chose, He would have put His sights on the doctors and the lawyers of His day.

It's not that it is bad to be knowledgeable, the problem lies in getting to a point where you rely more on knowledge than in faith to interpret God's will and to serve in His Kingdom.

When the believer abandons the concept of living by faith, he becomes reliant on knowledge alone and thus develops a tendency to rationalize the Gospel. This comes at the expense of abandoning faith, without which the Bible tells us is impossible to please God. Knowledge, degrees, and credentials become the yardstick by which worthiness and value in the kingdom of God is determined.

In such an environment, not even the words of Jesus Himself are accepted as the final word. No wonder there is so much confusion today, where even Jesus words are not safe as a source of authority. This is very similar to the religious leaders of Jesus' times. They had ritualized and rationalized the Scriptures to the point that not even Jesus Himself could convince most of them of their arrogance and grave error! This shows that it can be just as difficult to break off the chains of ignorance through self-imposed efforts, as to break away from the chains of intellectual arrogance and pride. There seems to be a feeling in some "Christian circles" that they know better than God! Academia, books, and men's self-appointed authorities, are quickly replacing the Bible as the only inerrant word and source of absolute divine truth. Everything is up for grabs!

PRAY

> *"I am the vine, you are the branches. He who abides in Me, and I in him, bears much fruit; for without Me you can do nothing."* (Jn. 15:5 NKJV)

Jesus said, *"Without Me you cannot do anything."* In the same passage, Jesus also compares our relationship to Him as being like branches attached to a tree. The branch owes its existence and health to the tree; which is Jesus. When the branch is not connected, it dries out and dies. Jesus says, it must be cut down. Thanks be to God for His grace and mercy! There is a certain disconnect from God when the church does not pray.

The nutrients that flow from the trunk to the branches stop flowing. One nutrient is the Word from our Master to our hearts as we communicate with Him. It is the invisible miracle of life that occurs when our hearts are open to His presence. As a chemical reaction occurs when the sun rays strike the surface of a leaf and life-sustaining oxygen and nutrients are produced through the process of photosynthesis, this is the similar effect of the radiance of His presence in our lives through prayer. You cannot adequately explain it, but it is wonderful!

How can you receive further instruction from God in the process of revival if the lines of communication are either nonexistent or are obstructed. With good reason, prayer is absolutely essential to the process of revival. The power of the life-saving blood of Jesus must flow again through the veins/branches in order for spiritual life to return.

Seek My Face

> *O God, you are my God, and I long for you. My whole being desires you; like a dry, worn-out, and waterless land, my soul is thirsty for You.* (Ps. 63:1 TEV)

How many people in the United States are seeking God's favor through repentance? How many in the church for that matter? The Scripture says of wisdom: *"I love those who love Me, and those who seek me find Me"* (Pr. 8:17). He who finds God has indeed found the true source of wisdom and riches! And what happens when you find the face of God? We come and stand in His presence and experience His blessing and favor.

Well, many men and women of God do that on a daily basis. But not necessarily for the reasons that the Scripture talks about in 11 Chronicles 7:14. God is dealing here with repentance. He is speaking about the situation when people have gone astray and are no longer seeking His face, in His presence.

Jesus opened the way at Calvary for us to come to the throne of God by His shed blood. What an awesome privilege! But many these days have seen fit to abandon the joy, blessing, beauty, and excitement of being in His presence for the things of the world. Can you imagine that? That is the reason why the LORD asked of our ancestors,

*Cross over to the coasts of Kittim and look, send to Kedar
and observe closely; see if there has ever been anything
like this: Has a nation ever changed its gods? (Yet they
are not gods at all.) But My people have exchanged their
Glory for worthless idols. Be appalled at this, O heavens,
and shudder with great horror," declares the LORD. "My
people have committed two sins: They have forsaken
Me, the spring of living water, and have dug their own
cisterns, broken cisterns that cannot hold water." (Jer.
2:10-13)*

Let me make something very clear here. It does not matter how a person has been misled to believe the contrary, there isn't a more impacting, enjoyable experience that being in the presence of the LORD. There is no substitute for God's presence. Period!

When you are able to find Him, and stand in His presence, then the truth about your fallen condition becomes very clear. Even a man of God such as Isaiah fell naked and sinful at His presence:

*"So I said: 'Woe is me, for I am undone! Because I am a
man of unclean lips, and I dwell in the midst of a people
of unclean lips; for my eyes have seen the King, the LORD
of hosts.'"* (Is. 6:5)

Seeking God's face is coming face to face with Him who loves you profoundly. It is returning to the Father who offers love, protection, and provision for you. He is the only One who has the authority to make things right for you in the critical area of sin. Seeking God's face should be a natural step for those who have truly repented and know they have been forgiven, because the greatest barrier to being in God's presence is sin.

TURNING FROM THEIR WICKED WAYS

*See to it that no one misses the grace of God and that
no bitter root grows up to cause trouble and defile many.*
(Heb. 12:15)

Repentance cannot be achieved by simply recognizing our sins and asking for forgiveness. There has to be a separation from sin. That separation has to be immediate and decisive. A line must be drawn in the sand, so to speak. As long as the sin persists, there is separation from God. His favor will be absent. America, that's what we need today—favor from God. We must depart from and stand against anything and everything that defies God's law. We must abandon our pretentious ways and approach God with humility and child-like faith. We must stop pretending that we have all the answers and ask God for clear direction.

THEN I WILL HEAR FROM HEAVEN

It must be terrible for a nation that has experienced God's favor for so long to fall from that favor. It must be so sad when a misguided, well-intentioned people pray but there is no answer. Many believers are becoming more aware of the move of God around the world today. When they compare it to the relative inertia in the spiritual realm in the area of miracles and supernatural manifestations, it is not difficult for them to conclude that something is amiss! People around the earth are hungry for God; they are desperate for Him. They seek Him out with a passion. And we hear regular reports of the magnificent spiritual exploits that God is causing in their midst as His miraculous power flows and works to reveal His pleasure. In Africa, people are coming to the LORD by the millions. This is happening because of the signs and wonders that God is doing there. God has heard the plight of a historically forgotten people, and He likes what He sees in their hearts as they come to Him for answers, and salvation, and healing.

In contrast, here in the United States, the best that many can do is to try to explain through complex theological theories how signs and wonders are a thing of the past. If that were true, then how can they explain the many miracles, signs, and wonders that are presently occurring throughout the world?

Could it be, as far as signs and wonders are concerned, that the doors of heaven have been shut for a lack of repentance in the church in our society today? Compared to other parts of the world, signs and wonders in the United States occur at the rate of a trickle. The gates of heaven need to be open, church, the gates of heaven need to be open in America!

THE ISSUE OF SIN

> *For the wages of sin is death, but the gift of God is eternal life in Christ Jesus our LORD.* (Rom. 6:23)

The forgiveness of sin is preceded by repentance and drawing close to God. It is followed by an outpouring of God's grace in the form of forgiveness and healing. That's because sin is a dangerous, deadly sickness of the soul that robs the individual of his health. Untreated, it can progress to the point of spiritual death.

Revival, the restoration of life in the individual and the body, cannot occur without healing. Healing cannot occur without repentance. Revival of the body, or the individual, once it has reached the point of death, cannot occur without resurrection power that accompanies forgiveness which only God can provide. He has made it available through the sacrifice of Christ on the cross.

These days we hear a great deal about the damage this generation and previous have inflicted on the environment. Greedy exploitation of the natural resources has left the planet in a serious condition. This situation, in turn, has provoked many new and dangerous illnesses to the body and the mind which were not even known to previous generations. During our lifetime, we have witnessed the appearance of countless diseases to the human population as well as to animals and plant life. One of the most powerful industries in the United States is the drug industry. It is continuously developing new chemical treatments in an attempt to keep up with the ever rising numbers of the sick and dying!

All this at a time when the church in the United States has declared itself bankrupt of supernatural power and seems powerless to heal the sick. It is no wonder that faith has taken a relegated and secondary position to medical treatment. Yet, if there has ever been a time when the miraculous power of the incomparable blood of Jesus was most needed, it is today. But how can that power work for healing in a generation that has denied its efficacy? Jesus, forgive us, heal us, and save us from ourselves!

The healing of the land also brings about prosperity. There cannot be a nation on the face of the earth that walks in God's favor and does not show visible signs of prosperity. A healthy individual is a prosperous individual. There is nothing more important to the enjoyment of God-given abundant life than the good health to enjoy it. Of course, the most important healing must occur first within the spirit of man. The forgiveness of sin brings about prosperity to the soul. The absence of sin returns the favor of God, first by salvation and also spiritual revival!

But God is also speaking of the literal earth. It is indisputable that our land is sick just as so many people living in it are as well, more than ever. One only needs to watch TV for a few minutes and to be bombarded by endless appeals for products that offer a healthier life. Countless politicians make their career promising a more responsible use of the resources and better health care. However, it is God's forgiveness that will bring about true healing!

Conclusion

So many times I have asked myself, "Why write a book about the vision now?" It has been nine years and two months, as I finish writing this book, since the vision was released in Minnesota and North Dakota. If it is God's will and purpose that this book is published, most people will become exposed to its contents for the first time during the year 2012. By then, it will have been ten years since the release of the vision. It would not take very long for even a cursory reader of the Holy Scriptures, to notice that God assigns important meanings to numbers. Here we have two key numbers, ten and twelve.

I always thought about this vision as all those years passed by. Certainly, some people have wondered if it would come to pass. Perhaps some have been skeptical about God's words and promises about this and have come to their own conclusions.

Consider what happened in the case of Abraham and Sarah. When Abraham was 75 years old, God made him a promise:

> "The LORD appeared to Abram and said, "To your offspring I will give this land." So he built an altar there to the LORD, Who had appeared to him." (Gen. 16:3)

But when he was 85, ten years later, God's promise remained unfulfilled. Therefore, Abraham devised himself a plan. Here how the story unfolds:

> But Abram said, "O Sovereign LORD, what can you gives me since I remain childless and the one who will

*inherit my estate is Eliezer of Damascus?" And Abram
said, "You have given me no children; so a servant in my
household will be my heir." Then the word of the LORD
came to him: "This man will not be your heir, but a son
coming from your own body will be your heir." He took
him outside and said, "Look up at the heavens and count
the stars—if indeed you can count them." Then He said
to him, "So shall your offspring be." Abram believed the
LORD, and He credited it to him as righteousness.* (Gen.
12:2-6)

Abraham complained that God had not moved fast enough
to fulfill His promise. Maybe he was getting a bit worried that
he was too old and nothing could happen. Ten years seemed to
him to be enough time for the promise to come to pass. Here is
the principle many of us often forget; God's thoughts are not
our thoughts:

*"For My thoughts are not your thoughts, neither are your
ways My ways," declares the LORD.* (Is. 55:8)

The LORD has His plan, and in due time, according to
His will, His promises will unfold before our very eyes. But
we must trust God's Word regardless of how hopeless the situ-
ation might look. Believing God (trusting and having faith in
His word) is what's going to bring us into right alignment with
His will.

But it does not end there. One year after God's reassur-
ance to Abraham, it was time for Sarah to get desperate:

*...So after Abram had been living in Canaan ten years,
Sarai his wife took her Egyptian maidservant Hagar and
gave her to her husband to be his wife.* (Gen. 16:3)

When Abraham was 86, Sarah (originally named Sarai)
suggested the idea of having Abraham sire a child by her maidservant, Hagar. But that did nothing to advance God's plan.
We cannot hurry or delay His plan. He will do as He pleases,
but He is always faithful to His promises! When man tries to
"help" God's plan, it simply demonstrates man's impatience

when things do not turn out the way he expects it or when he expects it. Very often, all our impatience produces are complications that can last a lifetime and beyond. Such were the results of Abraham's decision to put Sarah's plan into motion.

Yet, again, when Abraham was 99, or 13 years after the implementation of Sarah's ill-conceived plan, he once again asked God if Ishmael would become his inheritor. The answer was again in the negative. However, it was not until that point that God revealed to him more specifically when the true heir would arrive; exactly one year later when he was 100 years old!

The feeling in the air is that there is a shift taking place in our spiritual environment that is indicative of a mighty move of God that is about to explode in our midst. It is a feeling that many people share. Something is happening! God has set the stage. Behold, the Glory of God is about to shake up America like it has never seen before. The question is, "Can you believe?"